总顾问：牛 健 丁国声
总主编：任静生

# 职场综合英语教程

## （基础篇）

主 编：王文婷
副主编：赵 芳 祝 然
编 者：王 诚 汪江红 杨 柳
　　　　唐四保 郑礼常 梁利民

北京大学出版社
PEKING UNIVERSITY PRESS

图书在版编目(CIP)数据

职场综合英语教程(基础篇)/王文婷主编. —北京:北京大学出版社,2012.8
(全国职业技能英语系列教材)

ISBN 978-7-301-20743-7

Ⅰ.①职… Ⅱ.①王… Ⅲ.①英语-高等职业教育-教材 Ⅳ.①H31

中国版本图书馆CIP数据核字(2012)第118281号

| 书　　　　名：职场综合英语教程(基础篇)
| 著作责任者：王文婷　主编
| 策　　　划：谢尚楹　万晶晶
| 责　任　编　辑：郝妮娜
| 标　准　书　号：ISBN 978-7-301-20743-7/H·3065
| 出　版　发　行：北京大学出版社
| 地　　　　址：北京市海淀区成府路205号　100871
| 网　　　　址：http://www.pup.cn
| 电　　　　话：邮购部 62752015　发行部 62750672　编辑部 62759634　出版部 62754962
| 电　子　邮　箱：zbing@pup.pku.edu.cn
| 印　刷　者：北京大学印刷厂
| 经　销　者：新华书店
　　　　　　　787毫米×1092毫米　16开本　9.5印张　280千字
　　　　　　　2012年8月第1版　2015年7月第4次印刷
| 定　　　　价：38.00元(附光盘)

未经许可,不得以任何方式复制或抄袭本书之部分或全部内容。
版权所有,侵权必究　举报电话:010-62752024
　　　　　　　　　　　电子邮箱:fd@pup.pku.edu.cn

# 前　言

职业化已经成为高职高专教育最显著的特征。增加实训、强调动手能力、采用"订单式"培养模式是其主要特色。在这种背景下，按照传统的教学方法进行基础课教学已经不容置疑的受到了挑战。就目前情况论，高职高专的基础课教学必须践行"以服务为宗旨，以就业为导向"的专业建设指导思想。在课程建设以及基础课教学内容中，必须结合学生的专业需求，有意识地融入与职场相关联的知识。

根据教育部《高职高专英语教育课程教学基本要求》的精神，联合国家级示范高职院校和骨干高职院校的一线教师，在充分调查现有高职高专英语教材的基础上，结合高职英语教学的未来发展趋势，在"安徽省高职高专外语教研会"的组织及北京大学出版社的支持下，编写了本套《职场综合英语教程》，并被列入普通高等教育"十二五"规划教材。

本套教程分为基础篇、第一册、第二册和第三册，共四册。

**基础篇**　主要针对英语基础比较薄弱的学生，融入了对音标的训练，旨在帮助这部分学生巩固英语的基础知识，为后续课程的学习奠定必要的基础。

**第一册**　主要涉及西方文化和日常生活，内容涵盖西方名人、青年旅馆、主题公园、肥皂剧、网上购物等。鲜活的内容、生活化的主题，有利于学生顺利融入大学生活，同时也有助于培养学生对英语学习的兴趣，为今后的职业化过渡打下坚实基础。

**第二册**　主要涉及求职以及职业素养培养等主题，如求职、自主创业、职场中人际交往和做好服务、科技与生活、名人的成功与失败等。另外，本册内容与职场文化的有机融合有利于学生对未来职业规划形成初步的认识。

**第三册**　从职场生活出发，针对高职学生可能遇到的职场活动进行设计，内容包括机场接待、银行服务、汽车制造等。内容难度适中，选材谨慎，真正做到通识化与职场化有机统筹，有助于学生以后进一步学习相关的专业英语。

本套教材的内容主要分为六个方面：听说、阅读、语法、应用文写作、文化速递与拓展词汇。

**听说部分**　践行任务型教学的指导思想，强调能听懂简单对话，能记录关键词，能就所给事物说出英语名称，或进行角色分工，完成简单对话。这部分设计了热身环节，通过比较容易完成的任务，帮助学生尽快进入相关主题的学习。而角色扮演部分则试图充分调动学生的想象力和创造力,按照角色分工完成任务。听说部分还设计了听写内容,旨在培养学生听懂并记录关键词的能力。

**阅读部分** 由两篇相关主题的文章组成,其中第一篇为主要文章,教师应该进行精深讲解;第二篇属于附加文章,教师可以把它作为泛读教材使用。目的是让学生在阅读过程中完成对该主题的英语核心词汇的巩固和学习,同时深刻理解英语的语句结构。

**语法部分** 旨在夯实高职高专学生的语法基础,改善语法能力薄弱的现状,同时结合"高等学校英语应用能力考试"要求,对一些考试技巧进行精解,真正做到融会贯通,为提高英语综合能力打下良好基础。

**写作部分** 紧扣职场,重在应用文的写作。提供较规范的写作模式与常用句型供学生参考,通过实际的操练让学生进一步熟悉并掌握多种应用文的写作。

**文化速递** 是本套教材的特色之一。是针对单元主题的拓展性学习资料,可以帮助学生开阔视野、拓展知识面,提高综合人文素养。

**词汇部分** 依据大纲要求,课文中涉及的生词均分级标出。标★为A级词汇,标☆为超纲词汇。方便教师把握教学重点,也方便学生分级掌握词汇,逐步进级。

**配有教学课件** 每个单元针对不同的主题都有话题的进一步延伸,有利于教师进行拓展教学。丰富授课内容,活跃课堂气氛,激发学生的学习兴趣。

本套教材得到教育部高等学校高职高专英语类专业教学指导委员会的悉心指导,由教指委秘书长牛健博士和副主任委员丁国声教授担任总顾问,由安徽新华学院外国语学院院长任静生教授担任总主编,国家示范性高等职业院校芜湖职业技术学院、安徽水利水电职业技术学院、安徽职业技术学院、安庆职业技术学院等院校的英语教学专家负责编写任务;明尼苏达大学商业管理Brian Meyer博士以及天津外国语大学等院校的专家为此套教材的出版倾注了大量的心血;其他参编人员及编辑老师们也付出了巨大的努力,在此谨向他们表示衷心的感谢。

高职高专英语教学任重道远,教材建设未有止境。本套教材的出版旨在探索新形势下高职高专英语教学的一条教学新路。缺点与不足之处在所难免,衷心希望得到专家学者的批评指正,听到广大师生的改进意见。

编者<br>2012年5月

# Contents

**Unit 1　Campus Life** ........................................................... 1
- Part Ⅰ　Phonetics / 2
- Part Ⅱ　Listening and Speaking / 4
- Part Ⅲ　Reading / 8
   - Text A　*How to Save Money in University* / 8
   - Text B　*You Can Go Home Now Mom and Dad* / 12
- Part Ⅳ　Grammar 语法结构的层次 / 16
- Part Ⅴ　Applied Writing: Business Card (名片) / 18
- Part Ⅵ　Cultural Express: Habits of High Effective Students / 22

**Unit 2　Pop Music** ........................................................... 26
- Part Ⅰ　Phonetics / 27
- Part Ⅱ　Listening and Speaking / 29
- Part Ⅲ　Reading / 32
   - Text A　*How Adele Conquered the World* / 32
   - Text B　*Whitney Houston, "We Will Always Love You"* / 36
- Part Ⅳ　Grammar 句子结构 / 40
- Part Ⅴ　Applied Writing: Greeting Cards (贺卡) / 42
- Part Ⅵ　Cultural Express: Bruno Mars：Just the Way You Are / 45

**Unit 3　Sports** ........................................................... 48
- Part Ⅰ　Phonetics / 49
- Part Ⅱ　Listening and Speaking / 51
- Part Ⅲ　Reading / 54
   - Text A　*Why Olympians Must Seize the Moment* / 54
   - Text B　*Martial Ethics* / 58
- Part Ⅳ　Grammar 名词和代词 / 62
- Part Ⅴ　Applied Writing: Lost and Found (寻物启事与失物招领) / 67
- Part Ⅵ　Cultural Express: Ding Junhui, the Easy-going Snooker Superstar / 69

| Unit 4 | Food Culture | 74 |
|---|---|---|
| Part Ⅰ | Phonetics / 75 | |
| Part Ⅱ | Listening and Speaking / 77 | |
| Part Ⅲ | Reading / 81 | |
| | *Text A  Our Heritage* / 81 | |
| | *Text B  Made Like No Other* / 85 | |
| Part Ⅳ | Grammar 形容词和副词 / 89 | |
| Part Ⅴ | Applied Writing: Notes (便条) / 92 | |
| Part Ⅵ | Cultural Express: Pizza Hut / 94 | |

| Unit 5 | Movie | 97 |
|---|---|---|
| Part Ⅰ | Phonetics / 98 | |
| Part Ⅱ | Listening and Speaking / 100 | |
| Part Ⅲ | Reading / 104 | |
| | *Text A  Wizard Series Ends* / 104 | |
| | *Text B  I'd Like to Thank My Mother...* / 108 | |
| Part Ⅳ | Grammar 动词I: 动词的种类 / 112 | |
| Part Ⅴ | Applied Writing: Memo (备忘录) / 114 | |
| Part Ⅵ | Cultural Express: American "Panda" Movie Stirs Controversy / 116 | |

| Unit 6 | Mother and Child | 120 |
|---|---|---|
| Part Ⅰ | Phonetics / 121 | |
| Part Ⅱ | Listening and Speaking / 123 | |
| Part Ⅲ | Reading / 127 | |
| | *Text A  A True Gift of Love* / 127 | |
| | *Text B  The Meanest Mother* / 131 | |
| Part Ⅳ | Grammar 动词II: 动词的时态和语态 / 134 | |
| Part Ⅴ | Applied Writing: Letters (书信) / 140 | |
| Part Ⅵ | Cultural Express: Mystery of the White Gardenia /144 | |

# Unit 1

## Campus Life

**Learning Objectives:**

You are able to:

- Identify some basic sounds of letters
- Use the proper expressions to comment on campus life
- Know the level of grammatical structure
- Write business card

You are suggested to:

- Be familiar with campus life

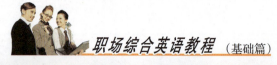

Campus life is not all about academics. It is much more than eating in the dining center and studying in the library. Experiences on campus are unique to every individual student. Their involvement in the diverse campus activities will foster their personal development and give them a sense of connection to student community. In this unit, students can find valuable tips on how to have a wonderful experience on campus and make their college experiences meaningful and productives, academically, financially and socially.

## Part I  Phonetics

### Task 1  Identifying Their Pronunciations

*Directions: Listen to the following words and read after the speaker, paying attention to the colored parts.*

| /iː/ | /ɪ/ | /ɛ/ | /a/ | /p/ |
| /b/ | /t/ | /d/ | /k/ | /g/ |

| | | | | |
|---|---|---|---|---|
| (1) seat | see | me | these | green |
| (2) list | this | finish | elect | country |
| (3) desk | pen | else | next | penny |
| (4) math | and | apple | thank | glad |
| (5) pen | apply | spell | people | pour |
| (6) brown | table | brother | beg | beer |
| (7) take | tour | towel | sit | site |
| (8) dad | good | deep | dean | dawn |
| (9) cake | black | can | club | look |
| (10) go | game | gate | bag | begin |

• Unit 1   Campus Life •

*Practice: Write down the sound of the underlined part of the words.*

tr<u>ee</u>    br<u>ea</u>d    cl<u>o</u>ck    r<u>i</u>ver    h<u>a</u>t

_____    _____    _____    _____    _____

## Task 2   Appreciating a Poem

*Directions: Listen to the poem "Never give up". Choose the words you hear to fill in the blanks.*

| allow | /əˈlaʊ/ | v. | 允许，许可（做某事） |
| cope | /kəʊp/ | v. | 成功地应付，对付 |
| patience | /ˈpeɪʃ(ə)ns/ | n. | 耐性，忍耐力，耐心 |
| strength | /streŋθ, streŋkθ/ | n. | 力量，体力，力气 |

| Poem | Never Give Up |
|---|---|

Never _____ (gave, give) up,
Never _____ (lose, loose) hope.
Always have _____ (face, faith),
It allows you to cope.
Trying times will _____ (path, pass),
As they always do.
Just have patience,
Your dreams will come true.
So put on a smile,
You'll _____ (live, leave) through your pain.
Know it will pass,
And strength you will _____ (gain, gained).

## Task3   Time for Fun: Tongue Twister

*Directions: Practise the tongue twister sentence by sentence after the speaker. Pay attention to the sounds.*

(1) I wish you were a fish in my dish.
(2) Knife and a fork, bottle and a cork, that is the way you spell New York.
(3) There is no need to light a night light at a light night like tonight for a bright night light is just like a slight light.

## Part II  Listening and Speaking

### Task 1  Short Dialogues

*Directions: Listen to the following short dialogues and fill in the blanks with the information you get from the recording. Each dialogue will be read twice.*

(1) **M:** What did your _____ tell you just now?
   **W:** He said that I should have _____ my report earlier.
(2) **M:** We finally _____, Mary!
   **W:** I can't believe _____ is tonight.
(3) **M:** Hi, did you pass your _____?
   **W:** Yeah, I did quite well. In fact, I got _____.
(4) **W:** The _____ is closed for repairs from the 1st of July till the 6th of August.
   **M:** Oh, my God! My library books are due on _____.
(5) **W:** Did Dr. Smith give a lecture on _____ in the hall last Friday?
   **M:** Yes, it's a _____ one.

### Task 2  Answering the Questions

*Directions: You will hear 5 recorded questions. Listen carefully and choose the proper answer to each question. The questions will be read twice.*

(1) A. Tom studies only at midnight.   B. Tom never studies.
   C. Tom seldom studies.   D. Tom studies only at the last possible moment.
(2) A. Chinese Dept. vs. Mathematics Dept.
   B. Computer Science Dept. vs. Chemistry Dept.
   C. Chinese Dept. vs. Chemistry Dept.
   D. Chinese Dept. vs. Foreign Languages Dept.
(3) A. Secretary and boss.   B. Student and teacher.
   C. Doctor and nurse.   D. Husband and wife.
(4) A. At 1:40.   B. At 1:50.
   C. At 2:00.   D. At 3:50.
(5) A. A New Year's concert.   B. A football match.
   C. A singing contest.   D. A dinner party.

## Task 3　Oral Practice

*Warm-Up 1: Match the expressions in the left column with the expressions in the right column so as to form 7 short dialogues.*

| | |
|---|---|
| (1) —What's today's assignment? | —I failed it. |
| (2) —When are we supposed to hand in our papers? | —Yes, I practice a lot every day. |
| (3) —You have made great progress in English. | —Read Chapter Ⅲ and discuss the following topics. |
| (4) —How do you like your music lessons? | —Thanks a lot. I'm so happy. |
| (5) —Are you on School's Basketball Team? | —By next Thursday. |
| (6) —What's the grade in your English exam? | —No, I'm a member of ELA. |
| (7) —Congratulations on your graduation! | —They are quite refreshing when we work so hard. |

*Warm-Up 2: Work with your partner to practise the following useful expressions.*

### If you are a teacher, you can say
(1) Today our job is to....
(2) Is it clear to you?
(3) Could you show us how to solve this problem?
(4) (name), what are you thinking about? It seems that you are wandering.
(5) Practice makes perfect. I suggest that you....
(6) You have made much progress in.... Keep on working hard!
(7) Don't worry. You still have time to...

### If you are a student, you can say
(1) Do you know what our required subjects are this semester?
(2) Professor..., could you explain the difference between...and....
(3) ...is too difficult for me. I don't know how to learn it well.
(4) I'm so pleased to know that I've passed the... exam.
(5) (name), would you like to join the ELA with me?
(6) Sir, can I borrow 6 books at a time?
(7) How fast time flies! We'll graduate in two weeks.

## Dialogue

*A is a teacher and B is a freshman. A is inquiring something of B.*

A: What attracted you to our university?

B: I like your sports facilities, especially the swimming pool.

A: Do you play many sports?

B: Yes, I like basketball and baseball.

A: Good, we have great teams here and you'll be able to try out for them. Where did you go to school before?

B: New Hope High School.

A: What did you take before?

B: English, Math, Biology, Chemistry and Computer.

A: Do you have your last report card?

B: Yes, here it is.

A: I see you got a "D" in Biology. How come?

B: Well, I found that subject hard.

A: Don't drop it. I think you could do that. I'll show you around the school now.

### New Words and Expressions

| attract | /əˈtrakt/ | v. | 吸引,引来 |
|---|---|---|---|
| facility | /fəˈsɪlɪti/ | n. | 设备,设施 |
| try out | | | 试验,选拔（尤指运动比赛或者角色甄选） |
| report card | | | 成绩单 |
| drop | /drɒp/ | v. | 落下,放弃 |
| show around | | | 陪同……参观 |

### Task 4　Role Play

(1) You and your classmate are talking about which university you would like to enter for. Make up a dialogue. The expressions given below may be of some help to you.

Unit 1  Campus Life

### Expressions

| | | | |
|---|---|---|---|
| prefer | /prɪˈfəː/ | v. | 宁可, 更喜欢 |
| enter for | | | 报名参加(比赛) |
| fame | /feɪm/ | n. | 名声, 名望 |
| campus | /ˈkampəs/ | n. | 校园, 场地 |
| faculty | /ˈfak(ə)lti/ | n | 全体教员 |

(2) You are asking your teacher about some information on further study. Make up a dialogue according to the information. The expressions given below may be of some help to you.

### Expressions

| | | | |
|---|---|---|---|
| go for further study | | | 考研, 进一步求学 |
| Internet | /ˈɪntənɛt/ | n. | 因特网 |
| catalogue | /ˈkat(ə)lɒg/ | n. | 目录, 总目 |
| a letter of recommendation | | | 推荐信 |
| apply for | | | 申请 |
| admission | /ədˈmɪʃ(ə)n/ | n. | 承认, 许可 |
| postgraduate | /pəʊs(t)ˈgradjʊət/ | n. | 研究生 |

## Task 5  Leisure Time: Learning to Sing a Song

1. Listen to the song "Scarborough Fair".
2. Listen to the song again and fill in the missing words.

**Scarborough Fair**

Are you going to Scarborough _____? Parsley, sage, rosemary and thyme. Remember me to one who lives there. She once was a true love of mine.

Tell her to make me a cambric _____. _____, parsley, sage, rosemary and thyme, without no seams nor needle work. Then she'll be a true love of mine.

Tell her to find me an acre of _____. _____, parsley, sage, rosemary and thyme, between the salt water and the sea strand. Then she'll be a true love of mine.

Tell her to reap it with a sickle of leather, parsley, sage, rosemary and thyme, and _____ it all in a bunch of heather. Then she'll be a true love of mine.

Are you going to Scarborough Fair? Parsley, sage, rosemary and thyme. _____ me to one who lives there. She once was a true love of mine.

3. Learn to sing the song after the singer.

## Part III  Reading

### Text A

### How to Save Money in University

There are many costs involved with going to college including tuition, books, housing, entertainment, and food. These costs can quickly add up and make life after college a financial nightmare. To avoid getting into a sticky situation yourself, here are five practical money tips for you, the college student.

**1. Be careful of promotions on campus.**

There are certain companies and organizations that make money by taking in inexperienced college students. Just be aware of the people out there hoping to make an easy dollar off you. Regardless of the tempting advertisements, read the fine print(小字体的附属条款).

**2. Don't eat out all the time.**

It may be convenient to eat out frequently, but it can end up costing you a lot of money. Start keeping track of how many times you eat out every week or month, to see how the costs add up. You might be surprised by how much money you spend on food.

**3. Use your credit card for emergencies only.**

With all of the expenses associated with going to college, it can be very easy to add up to a lot of credit card debt. So save it for emergencies only. It is easy to overspend and spend without thinking when you're paying with credit card, but when you pay with cash, things are very different.

**4. Buy books online before the semester starts.**

The profit rates at college and university bookstores can be as high as 50%. The main reason why students buy from these book stores is because of convenience, but the costs are just too high. If you plan ahead and buy your books online, you can save yourself hundreds of dollars per semester.

**5. Max out financial aid and scholarship.**

Find financial aid and scholarship programs to help pay for your education and other expenses. There is probably a scholarship program for your particular major, ethnic group, or background. Most of these scholarships require a simple essay and resume and can be well worth the time and effort put into applying for them.

# Unit 1  Campus Life

## New Words

| | | | | |
|---|---|---|---|---|
| ★ tuition | /tjuːˈɪʃ(ə)n/ | | n. | 学费 |
| housing | /ˈhaʊzɪŋ/ | | n. | 住房 |
| ☆ entertainment | /ˌɛntəˈteɪnm(ə)nt/ | | n. | 娱乐 |
| financial | /fʌɪˈnanʃ(ə)l, fɪ-/ | | a. | 金融的，经济的 |
| ☆ nightmare | /ˈnʌɪtmɛː/ | | n. | 恶梦 |
| avoid | /əˈvɔɪd/ | | v. | 避开，避免，预防 |
| sticky | /ˈstɪki/ | | adj. | （状况）为难的，尴尬的 |
| practical | /ˈpraktɪk(ə)l/ | | a. | 实际的 |
| ★ tip | /tɪp/ | | n. | 建议，小贴士 |
| ☆ promotion | /prəˈməʊʃn/ | | n. | 促销 |
| inexperienced | /ˌɪnɛkˈspɪərɪənst, ˌɪnɪkˈspɪərɪənst/ | | adj. | 缺少经验的 |
| aware | /əˈwɛː/ | | adj. | 知道的，意识到的 |
| tempt | /tɛm(p)t/ | | v. | 诱惑 |
| ★ regardless | /rɪˈɡɑːdlɪs/ | | adv. | 不管怎样 |
| ☆ emergency | /ɪˈməːdʒ(ə)nsi/ | | n. | 紧急状况 |
| expense | /ɪkˈspɛns, ɛk-/ | | n. | 费用，经费 |
| ☆ overspend | /əʊvəˈspɛnd/ | | v. | 透支 |
| ahead | /əˈhɛd/ | | adv. | 事先，提前 |
| ★ scholarship | /ˈskɒləʃɪp/ | | n. | 奖学金 |
| major | /ˈmeɪdʒə/ | | n. | 专业 |
| ethnic | /ˈɛθnɪk/ | | a. | 种族的 |
| ☆ essay | /ˈɛseɪ/ | | n. | 论文，短文 |
| resume | /rɪˈzjuːm/ | | n. | 简历 |

## Phrases and Expressions

| | |
|---|---|
| involved with | 涉及，与……有关联 |
| take in | 欺骗 |
| be aware of | 意识到 |
| regardless of | 尽管，无论 |
| eat out | 外出吃饭 |
| end up doing | 结果…… |
| associated with | 和……有关 |
| add up to | 共计 |
| financial aid | 财政援助贷款 |
| apply for | 申请 |

9

# Exercises

*Directions: Answer the following questions according to the passage.*

1. What are costs involved with going to college?
2. How many suggestions are mentioned to avoid a sticky situation?
3. What's the purpose of promotions on campus?
4. Who are easier to be taken in by promotions on campus, freshmen or seniors?
5. What might be the problem with using credit card?
6. Why do students choose to buy books at college and university bookstores?
7. Is scholarship available only for excellent students?
8. If a college student applies for scholarship, what should he or she prepare for?

*Directions: Choose the best meaning of each italicized word according to the context and try to tell how you get the answer.*

1. To avoid getting into a sticky situation yourself, here are five practical money *tips* for you, the college student.
   A. 尖端　　B. 小费　　C. 建议
2. There are certain companies and organizations that make money by *taking in* inexperienced college students.
   A. 吸收　　B. 引进　　C. 欺骗
3. With all of the expenses associated with going to college, it can be very easy to *add up to* a lot of credit cards.
   A. 加到　　B. 加起来　　C. 总计
4. If you plan *ahead* and buy your books online, you can save yourself hundreds of dollars per semester.
   A. 在前方　　B. 提前　　C. 领先
5. The profit *rates* at college and university bookstores are as high as 50%.
   A. 速度　　B. 比率　　C. 范围

## Unit 1  Campus Life

## Vocabulary

*Directions:* Match each word in column A with its definition in Column B

| Column A | Column B |
|---|---|
| 1. nightmare | a. difficult, dangerous; causing problems |
| 2. tuition | b. an unexpected and dangerous situation to be dealt with immediately |
| 3. housing | c. things intended to amuse or interest people |
| 4. sticky | d. to spend more money than you can afford |
| 5. inexperienced | e. the money you pay for being taught |
| 6. overspend | f. reach a maximum |
| 7. emergency | g. the houses or conditions that people live in |
| 8. max out | h. money to give someone to help pay for their education |
| 9. scholarship | i. a very frightening dream |
| 10. entertainment | j. not having much experience of life |

*Directions:* Complete the following sentences with words from Column A above. Change the forms where necessary.

1. When I started college, the _____ was only $ 350 each quarter.
2. Nowadays many young people _____ their income and often borrow money from parents.
3. Some health problems are caused by bad _____.
4. The staff needs to know what to do in an _____.
5. He applied for an American university on a considerable _____.
6. On average, the downtown provides a variety of _____.
7. Because of new regulations, some estates are in a _____ situation.
8. The car _____ at 150 mph.
9. Jim can be so _____ that he believes good things will always happen.
10. Years after the accident, I still have _____ _____ about it.

*Directions:* Translate the following sentences into English.

1. Buying a car _____ (包括支付) its insurances and maintenance.
2. Why do some students with high IQ _____ _____ (结果却考试不及格)?
3. She _____ (已经感受到了) the stress from city life.
4. _____ (尽管) a recent operation, he continued his work.
5. We _____ (只是把所有的数加起来) and divided one by another.
6. Some college students do part-time jobs in their spare time to _____ (挣钱).
7. The machines exported from Japan are in high quality but _____ (就是价格太高).
8. He left _____ (没有跟我说一句话).

### Text B

## You Can Go Home Now Mom and Dad

In order to separate doting parents from their freshman sons, Morehouse College in Atlanta has held a formal "Parting Ceremony".

It began on a recent evening, with speeches in the Martin Luther King Jr. International Chapel. Then the incoming freshmen marched through the gates of the campus — which swung shut, symbolically leaving the parents outside.

Grinnell College here, like others, has found it necessary to be clear about when parents really, truly must say goodbye. After baggage had been carried to dorm rooms, everyone gathered in the gymnasium, students on one side of the bleachers, parents on the other.

Moving their students in usually takes a few hours. Moving on? Most deans can tell stories of parents who lingered around campus for days. At Colgate University, "a mother and father once went to their daughter's classes on the first day of the semester and came to the registrar's office to change her schedule", recalled Beverly Low, the dean of first-year students. "We recognize it's a huge day for families," she said.

A more common way is for colleges to introduce blunt language into schedules specifying the hour for last hugs. As of 5:30 p.m. on Sept. 11, for example, the parents of Princeton freshmen learn from the move-in schedule, "following orientation events are intended for students only". The language was added in recent years to draw a clear line. It's easy for students to point to this statement and say "Hey, Mom, I think you're supposed to be gone now".

(*New York Times*, August 31, 2010)

## Unit 1  Campus Life

### New Words

| | | | |
|---|---|---|---|
| doting | /ˈdəʊtɪŋ/ | adj. | 溺爱孩子的 |
| hold | /həʊld/ | v. | 举办 |
| march | /mɑːtʃ/ | v. | 步行 |
| symbolical | /sɪmˈbɒlɪkl/ | adj. | 象征性的 |
| ★gymnasium | /dʒɪmˈneɪzɪəm/ | n. | 体育馆 |
| ☆bleachers | /ˈbliːtʃəz/ | n. | 露天看台 |
| dean | /diːn/ | n. | 院长 |
| linger | /ˈlɪŋɡə/ | v. | 逗留 |
| ★semester | /sɪˈmɛstə/ | n. | 学期 |
| schedule | /ˈʃɛdjuːl, ˈskɛd-/ | n. | 课程表 |
| recall | /rɪˈkɔːl/ | v. | 回忆 |
| ☆recognize | /ˈrɛkəɡnʌɪz/ | v. | 意识到，认识到 |
| blunt | /blʌnt/ | adj. | 直言不讳的 |
| specify | /ˈspɛsɪfʌɪ/ | v. | 指定 |
| following | /ˈfɒləʊɪŋ/ | adj. | 此后的，随后的 |
| statement | /ˈsteɪtm(ə)nt/ | n. | 声明，陈述 |

### Phrases and Expressions

| | |
|---|---|
| separate ...from | (使)分开，分离 |
| Parting Ceremony | 分别仪式 |
| registrar's office | 注册办公室 |
| orientation events | 迎新活动 |
| point to | 提出，指出 |
| be supposed to... | 应该…… |

### Proper Names

| | | | |
|---|---|---|---|
| Morehouse College | | | 莫尔豪斯学院 |
| Atlanta | /ətˈlantə/ | n. | 亚特兰大(美国佐治亚州首府) |
| Martin Luther King Jr. International Chapel | | | 马丁·路德·金国际礼堂 |
| Grinnell College | | | 格林内尔学院 |
| Colgate University | | | 科尔盖特大学 |
| Princeton | /ˈprɪnstən/ | n. | 普林斯顿 |

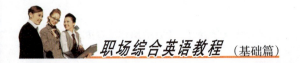

# Exercises

*Directions: Decide whether the following statements are true (T) or false (F) according to the information in the passage.*

1. According to the passage, parents are often reluctant to leave the children of university. ( )
2. Recently, many colleges have found it unnecessary to be clear about when parents must say goodbye. ( )
3. In order to improve the children's independence, parents should leave as soon as possible after sending their children to school. ( )
4. Freshmen tend to be sad if their parents are refused to participate in orientation activities. ( )
5. According to Beverly Low, some parents interfered in their children too much. ( )
6. A better approach for the school is to indicate the time when parents should leave school in the admission notice. ( )

*Directions: Guess the meanings of the words and phrases in the box according to the passage. Then, use them to complete the following sentences, changing the form if necessary.*

| be supposed to | point to | recognize | specify |
| separate from | linger | in order to | following |

1. _____ get a complete picture, you need further information.
2. In our country, people _____ shake hands when they meet someone for the first time.
3. He _____ the spot where the house used to stand.
4. She _____ for a few minutes after class to talk to the student.
5. The regulations _____ that calculators may not be used in the examination.
6. It is impossible to _____ belief _____ emotion.
7. The _____ event confirmed our doubts.
8. Nobody _____ how urgent the situation was.

*Directions: Pay attention to different parts of speech and select the appropriate word to fill in the blanks.*

1. entertain  entertainer  entertainment  entertaining
   a. He is a street _____.
   b. She was always so funny and _____.
   c. He _____ us for hours with his stories and jokes.
   d. The _____ was provided by a folk band.
2. differ  different  difference  differently
   a. There is no _____ in the results.
   b. French and English _____ in this respect.

c. Boys and girls may behave _____.
d. People often give very _____ accounts of the same event.

3. expense    expensive    expensively    inexpensive
   a. I can't afford it, it's too _____.
   b. She always travels first-class regardless of _____.
   c. In order to save money, he went to a relatively _____ hotel.
   d. There are other restaurants where you can eat less _____.

4. convenient    convenience    inconvenient    inconvenience
   a. The position of the house combines quietness and _____.
   b. That's most _____ for me. I'm working that weekend.
   c. It's very _____ to pay by credit card.
   d. We apologize for the delay and regret any _____ it may have caused.

*Directions: First translate the following sentences into Chinese. Then, pay attention to the italicized (斜体的) parts in the English sentences and translate the Chinese sentences by simulating the structure of the English sentences.*

1. *In order to* separate doting parents from their freshman sons, Morehouse College in Atlanta has held a formal "Parting Ceremony".
   她早早到场，想找个好位置。

2. It began on a recent evening, *with* speeches in the Martin Luther King Jr. International Chapel.
   站着的时候别把双手插在口袋里。

3. Then the incoming freshmen marched *through* the gates of the campus.
   这条小路穿过树林通向河边。

4. Grinnell College here, like others, has *found it* necessary *to* be clear about when parents really, truly must say goodbye.
   我发现很难听懂老师上课所讲的内容。

5. *Moving* their students in usually *takes* a few hours.
   学习语法是学习一门语言的好方法。

6. Following orientation events *are intended for* students only.
   这本书是为儿童写的。

7. *It's easy for* students *to* point to this statement and say goodbye to their parents.
   对外国人来说使用筷子可不是一件容易的事。

8. I think you're *supposed to* be gone now.
   我应该7点到达，但我8点才到。

*Directions: Group activity.*

1. You are a freshman of the college. Are you a bit uncertain about your new life? How are you feeling? Which of the following adjectives could apply to you? Why?

   a. nervous     b. thrilled     c. apprehensive
   
   d. cheerful    e. anxious      f. miserable

2. Do you have any suggestions for your classmates to solve their problems if they don't adapt themselves to the new campus life?

## Part IV  Grammar

## 语法结构的层次

英语语法结构具有层次性,由小到大分为五个不同层次。它们是:词素(morpheme)、词(word)、词组(phrase)、分句(clause)和句子(sentence)。通过句子层次图可以清楚知道句子的构成:

### 一、词素

词素(morpheme)是最小的载有语义的单位,也是最小的语法单位。词素可分为自由词素和黏着词素。

**1. 自由词素(Free Morpheme)**

自由词素意义基本完整,可单独成词,如:it, make, man, harm, fast 等。自由词素常可作为词根(root),它同附着在它身上的词缀(affix)一起组成派生词(derivative word),如:

happy: *un*happy, happi*ly*, happi*ness*, *un*happi*ly*

care: care*less*, care*ful*, care*fully*

自由词素还可同其他自由词素构成复合词(compound word)，如：

straw: strawberry, straw-board, strawworm

finger: fingerling, fingerprint, fingertip

### 2. 黏着词素 (Bound Morpheme)

黏着词素本身意义不够完整，也不可单独成词，如：un-, a-, -ful, -er, -ing 等。黏着词素黏附在自由词素上，表现为前缀和后缀，可以形成具有新的语义或新的语法意义的词，如：

| 前缀 | 后缀 |
|---|---|
| un-happy | harm-ful |
| il-logical | move-ment |
| co-exist | go-ing |
| anti-Japanese | fan-s |

黏着词素又可进一步分为屈折性词素(inflectional)和派生性词素(derivational)。词根加上屈折性词素不会产生新词，但会发生语法意义上的变化，如：

-s: Henry*s*, studi*es*        -ed: confirm*ed*, rel*ated*

通过加上派生性词素，常可产生新词，如：

-er: play*er*, teenag*er*        un-: *un*acceptable, *un*like

**常用前缀：**

| un- | non- | in- | dis- | counter- | anti- | de- |
|---|---|---|---|---|---|---|
| super- | over- | under- | semi- | mini- | | |
| pre- | fore- | post- | sub- | inter- | trans- | |
| be- | en- | a- | | | | |

**常用后缀：**

| -ation | -ment | -al | -ness | -ity | -ism | |
|---|---|---|---|---|---|---|
| -er | -ee | -ist | -age | | | |
| -y | -ish | -some | -ous | -ly | -ize | -en | -ify |
| -s | -'s | -ed | -ing | -est | | |

## 二、词、词组

根据词法，英语中词可以分为简单词、派生词和复合词。

1. 简单词是由一个自由词素构成的词，如：go，down，new 等。

    派生词是由词根加派生性黏着词素构成的，如：de-duct，mis-judge，train-ee 等。

    复合词由两个或以上自由词素构成，如：tooth-pick，mass-produce，more-over 等。

2. 词组通常是两个或两个以上的词组成的语法单位。词组的中心词是什么，就叫做什么词组，如：pretty difficult，full enough 等，中心词是形容词，故叫做形容词词组。

17

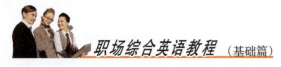

### 三、分句、句子

分句是一个"主语+谓语"的结构，语义完整。独立分句不依赖其他结构而单独存在，就形成句子，如：Nobody knows everything about the world. 从属分句以句子的一个成分的形式出现，如：I can't remember who locked the door. 句子是人们表达思想进行交际的基本语言单位。当句子只包括一个分句时，句子和分句是没有区别的。

## Exercises

*Directions: Point out the following word morpheme.*（指出下面单词的词素）

| | | | | |
|---|---|---|---|---|
| unlucky | kilometer | multimedia | married | shining |
| dislike | carelessness | postwar | childhood | give |

*Directions: Combine the following 12 words to form six compound words.*（将下面十二个单词组合成六个复合词）

door, guide, news, head, book, light, hand, moon, bell, teacher, paper, bag

*Directions: Judge the sentence elements of the underlined part.*（判断句子划线部分的句子成分）

1) The tall boy sitting in the corner is my brother.
2) The course is pretty difficult.
3) He spoke loudly and clearly.
4) We're collecting money for the benefit of some orphans.
5) What you said is not true.
6) Hungry and exhausted, the climbers returned.
7) I signed the paper to get the license.
8) He knows everything about it.
9) He found it important to master English.
10) What a beautiful Chinese painting it is!

## Part V  Applied Writing

### Business Card (名片)

名片通常用于社交场合，用来向他人介绍自己的姓名和身份。在国际商务活动中，交换名片是一项很流行、也很重要的礼仪。一般名片上的信息包括以下几部分：(1) 单位(公司)名称(the name of company)；(2) 本人姓名(person's name)；(3) 职位、职称、头衔(position, title)；(4) 联系方式(地址 the address of your company、电话号码 telephone number、传真号码

Unit 1　Campus Life

fax number、电子邮箱等 E-mail address）。名片中各项内容的位置可作适当调整。

【格式】

```
Organization
                        Name
                        Title



Address:
E-mail:
Tel:
Mobile phone:
```

Sample 1:

```
              乔治·瓦茨 教授
              爱丁堡内皮尔大学
                   校长


英国苏格兰爱丁堡   克林顿大街20 号   曼彻斯顿校园
电话 0044 544××××
传真 0044 544××××
```

```
           PROFESSOR GEORGE WATTS
                   PRINCIPAL
                NAPIER UNIVERSITY
                    EDINBURGH


MERCHISTON CAMPUS. 20 COLINTON ROAD
EDINBURGH, SCOTLAND.UK
TEL: 0044 544××××    FAX: 0044 544××××
```

**Sample 2:**

美国驻华大使馆美国教育交流中心

陈顺达

主 任

北京朝阳区呼家楼
京广中心××××
邮编：100020

电话：(010)3572-××××转××××
传真：(010)3572-××××
电子邮件：csd××@yahoo.com.cn

Embassy of the United States of America
American Center for Educational Exchange

**Shunda Chen**

Director

Suite××××, Jingguang Center
Hujialou, Chaoyang District
Beijing 100020

Tel：(010)3572-××××Ext.××××
Fax：(010)3572-××××
E-mail：csd××@yahoo.com.cn

**注意事项：**

1. 关于地名的写法，一般遵循从小地名到大地名的写法。
   一般顺序为：室号—门牌号—街道名—城市名—省(州)—国家
   Room ×× No. ×× ××× Road (Street)
   ×× City ×× Province ××××××(邮编)
   ××× (country)

2. 地址在名片上，应该保持一定的完整性。门牌号与街道名不可分开写，必须在同一行，不可断行。各种名称不可断开。

3. 门牌号英美写法可有不同，如：英语写No. 26, 美语可写26#

4. 汉语的人名，地名一般写汉语拼音。有些译法可以不同：如中山东路，可以译为 Zhongshan East Road 也可译为 Zhongshan Donglu Road 但像一些地名，如南天门，香南路，就应该直写拼音，而不能将其中某个字译为英语。即：Nantianmen, Xiangnan Road 而不是 South Tianmen, Xiang South Road。

# Unit 1  Campus Life

## Basic Expressions（常用表达）

◆ 常见部门

　　☆Board of Directors 董事会
　　☆General Manager Office 总经理办公室
　　☆Administrative Dept. 行政管理办公室
　　☆Personnel Dept. 人事部
　　☆Human Resources Dept. 人力资源部

◆ 常见职位表达法

1. 副

　　（1）Vice-　　　Vice Chairman 副主席　　Vice President 副总裁
　　（2）Deputy-　　Deputy Director 副主任　Deputy Secretary-general 副秘书长
　　　（注：主要用来表示企业、事业、行政部门的副职）
　　（3）Assistant-　Assistant Manager 副经理　Assistant Engineer 助理工程师
　　　（注：主要强调"助理"的含义）
　　（4）Associate-　Associate Professor 副教授　Associate Research Fellows 副研究员
　　　（注：常用于表示技术职称的副职）

2. 兼

　　"and"，如：
　　Chairman of the Board of Directors and Chief Executive Officer 董事长兼首席执行官

3. 名誉

　　"Honorary" or "Emeritus"，如：
　　Honorary Chairman 名誉主席　　　　　Emeritus President 名誉校长

◆ 联系地址常用词语

Road (Rd.) 路　　　　　　　　　　　　Street (St.) 街
Lane 弄，里　　　　　　　　　　　　　Alley 胡同
Residential Area/ Quarter 新村，小区　　Avenue (Av.) 大道
Floor (Fl.) 楼　　　　　　　　　　　　Building (Bldg.) 大楼
Room (Rm.) 室　　　　　　　　　　　　Apartment (Apt.) 公寓
Corporation (Corp.) 公司　　　　　　　Company (Co.) 公司
Incorporated (Inc.) 有限的　　　　　　Company Limited (Co., Ltd.) 有限公司
Address (Add.) 地址

◆ 联系方式常用词语

Telephone (Tel.) 电话　　　　　　　　Home phone (H.) 住宅电话
Office phone (O.) 办公室电话　　　　　Teletype exchange (Telex.) 电传
Mobile phone (M.P.) 手机

## Exercises

*Directions: This part is to test your ability to do practical writing. You are required to put the following card into English.*

---

**广东省青青源茶业有限公司**

赵国栋　副总经理

地址：中国广东惠州市隆平高科技园青青源科技产业区
电话：0752-26536××　　手机：1393231××××
传真：0752-26536××　　电子邮件：zdg××@163.com
网址：www.qingqingyuan.com　　邮编：210125

---

## Part VI  Cultural Express

### Habits of High Effective Students
*Suresh*

Some people believe that really successful students are just born that way. True, some students are able to breeze through school with little or no effort. However, the most of successful students achieve their success by developing and applying effective study habits. The following are the top 10 study habits employed by highly successful students. So if you want to become a successful student, don't get discouraged, don't give up, just work to develop each of the study habits below and you'll see your grades go up, your knowledge increase and your ability to learn and assimilate information improve.

**1. Don't try cram all your studying into one session.**

Successful students typically space their work out over shorter periods of time and rarely try to cram all of their studying into just one or two sessions. If you want to become a successful student then you need to learn to be consistent in your studies and to have regular, yet shorter, study periods.

**2. Plan when you're going to study.**

Successful students schedule specific times throughout the week when they are going to complete their studying and then they stick with their schedule. Students who study irregularly typically do not perform as well as students who have a set study schedule.

### 3. Study at the same time.

Not only is it important that you plan when you're going to study but that you also create a consistent, daily study routine. When you study at the same time each day and each week your studying will become a regular part of your life. You'll be mentally and emotionally more prepared for each study session and each study session will become more productive.

### 4. Each study time should have a specific goal.

Simply studying without direction is not effective. You need to know exactly what you need to accomplish during each study period. Before you start studying, set a study period goal that supports your overall academic goal, for example, memorize 30 vocabulary words in order to prepare for the upcoming vocabulary test.

### 5. Never delay your planned study session.

It's very easy, and common, to put off your study time because of lack of interest in the subject, because you have other things you need to get done first or just because the homework is hard. Successful students DO NOT delay studying. If you delay your study period, your studying will become much less effective and you may not get everything accomplished that you need to. Delay also leads to rushing, and rushing is the number one cause of errors.

### 6. Start with the most difficult subject first.

As your most difficult homework or subject will require the most effort and mental energy you should start with it first. Once you've completed the most difficult work it will be much easy to finish the rest of your work. Believe it or not, starting with the most difficult work will greatly improve the effectiveness of your study period and your academic performance.

### 7. Always review your notes before starting an assignment.

Obviously, before you can review your notes you must first have notes. Always make sure to take good notes in class. Before you start each study session and before you start a particular assignment, review your notes thoroughly to make sure you know how to complete the assignment correctly.

### 8. Make sure you're not disturbed while you're studying.

When you're disturbed while you're studying you (1) lose your train of thought and (2) you get distracted—both of which will lead to very ineffective studying. Before you start studying find a place where you won't be disturbed.

### 9. Use study groups effectively.

Have you ever heard the phrase "two heads are better than one"? Well this can be especially true when it comes to studying. Working in groups enables you to (1) get help from other students when you're struggling to understand a concept, (2) complete assignments more quickly, and (3) teach others whereby helping both the other students and yourself to better understand the subject matter. However, study groups can become very ineffective if they're not structured and if group members come unprepared. Effective students use study groups effectively.

**10. Review your notes, schoolwork and other class materials over the weekend.**

Successful students review what they've learned during the week and over the weekend. This way they're well prepared to continue learning new concepts at the beginning of each week that build upon previous coursework and knowledge learned the previous week.

We're confident that if you'll develop the habits outlined above that you'll see a major improvement in your academic success.

## 拓展词汇

### 人物

president 校长; faculty 教职工总称; professor 教授; associate professor 副教授; lecturer 讲师; assistant professor 助教; undergraduate 本科生; postgraduate 研究生; graduate 毕业生; advisor 导师; counselor 辅导老师; alumni 校友; a grand-aided student 领取助学金的学生; auditor 旁听生; boarder 住宿生

### 学习

score 成绩; credit 学分; program 某一专业的课程总称; degree 学位; selective/optional course 选修课; required/compulsory course 必修课; assignment 作业; project 学生独立完成的课外课题; handout 老师上课发的印刷品; participation 出勤; assessment 评估; presentation 针对某一专题进行的发言; lecture 老师的讲课; internship 实习; office hour 老师与学生面谈的时间; letter of recommendation 推荐信; paper/thesis/dissertation 论文/硕士论文/博士论文; open-book exam 开卷考试; report card 成绩单; final examination 期末考试；quiz 小测试；associate diploma 专科证书；bachelor 本科学位

### 机构

technical school 技校；Polytechnic Institute 理科学院；Open University 夜大，函授；Administration Office 行政办公室；School of Arts and Sciences 文理学院；International Student Office 留学生处；Security Office 安全管理处；Admissions Office 招生办；Students' Union 学生会；Students' Club 学生俱乐部

### 设施

canteen 餐厅；dining hall 食堂；cafeteria 自助小餐厅；dorm 宿舍；student hostel 学生公寓；teaching building 教学楼；lecture theatre 大教室，阶梯教室；auditorium 大礼堂；laboratory/lab 实验室；gymnasium 体育馆；teaching facilities 教学设施

### 生活

room and board 食宿；accommodation 住宿；open an account 开户；student account 银行中的学生账户；withdraw cash 取现金；deposit money in a bank 存钱；dormitory deposit 宿舍保证金；miscellaneous expenses 杂费

### 活动

enrollment 报到；orientation meeting 介绍会；open ceremony 开学典礼；after-school activities 课外活动；social investigation 社会调查；voluntary labor 义务劳动；campus job fairs 校园招聘会；graduation appraisal 毕业评估；graduation ceremony 毕业典礼

# Unit 2

## Pop Music

**Learning Objectives:**

You are able to:
- ☞ Identify some basic sounds of letters
- ☞ Use the proper expressions to comment on pop music
- ☞ Know the sentence structures
- ☞ Write greeting cards

You are suggested to:
- ☞ Be familiar with some pop music culture

# Unit 2　Pop Music

　　Pop music is a genre of music which originated in the 1950s, deriving from rock and roll. Pop music, as a genre, often borrows elements from other styles such as urban, dance, rock, Latin and country. It often uses such instruments as electric guitars, drums and a bass. In the case of such music, the main goal is usually that of being pleasurable to listen to rather than having much artistic depth. Pop music generally desires to appeal to a mass audience. This unit aims to introduce pop music and some popular singers, hoping to achieve a goal of broadening readers' mind.

## Part I　Phonetics

### Task 1　Identifying Their Pronunciations

*Directions: Listen to the following words and read after the speaker, paying attention to the colored parts.*

| /ʊ/ | /u:/ | /ɒ/ | /ɔ:/ | /ə/ |
|---|---|---|---|---|
| /ə:/ | /f/ | /v/ | /s/ | /z/ |

| | | | | |
|---|---|---|---|---|
| (1) put | look | woman | book | foot |
| (2) ruler | do | shoe | broom | too |
| (3) box | of | sorry | not | on |
| (4) forty | four | ball | daughter | your |
| (5) about | brother | today | parent | color |
| (6) learn | her | survey | shirt | term |
| (7) fare | soft | phase | photo | find |
| (8) have | very | over | seven | video |
| (9) class | stay | nice | license | pencil |
| (10) zero | these | hers | zoo | zone |

**Practice:** Write down the sound of the underlined part of the words.

b<u>ir</u>d     n<u>ur</u>se     sch<u>oo</u>l     w<u>a</u>tch     dog<u>s</u>

## Task 2  Appreciating a poem

*Directions: Listen to a poem "Life". Choose the words you hear to fill in the blanks.*

| cheerful | /ˈtʃɪəfʊl, -f(ə)l/ | adj. | 欢乐的, 高兴的 |
| painful | /ˈpeɪnfʊl, -f(ə)l/ | adj. | 痛苦的, 费力的, 伤脑筋的 |
| beautiful | /ˈbjuːtɪfʊl, -f(ə)l/ | adj. | 美丽的, 悦目的, 极好的 |

**Poem     Life**

Life can be good,
Life can be _____ (bad, bed),
Life is _____ (most, mostly) cheerful,
But sometimes _____ (said, sad).
Life can be dirty,
Life can even be painful,
But life is what you _____ (make, mark) it,
So _____ (trial, try) to make it beautiful.

## Task 3  Time for Fun: Tongue Twister

*Directions: Practise the tongue twister sentence by sentence after the speaker. Pay attention to the sounds.*

(1) Double bubble gum bubbles double.
(2) A big black bug bit a big black bear and made the big black bear bleed blood.
(3) While we were walking, we were watching window washers wash Washington's windows with warm washing water.

# Part II  Listening and Speaking

## Task 1  Short Dialogues

*Directions: Listen to the following short dialogues and fill in the blanks with the information you get from the recording. Each dialogue will be read twice.*

(1) **M:** I have _____ many classic songs from this website, such as "My Heart Will Go On", "When You Believe" and so on.
   **W:** Amazing! I'm always _____ to download the two songs.
(2) **M:** Do you love _____?
   **W:** Of course. I always listen to pop songs while ____ home.
(3) **M:** Are you going to the free _____ in the college hall this weekend?
   **W:** Sure. I'm not going to miss the good _____.
(4) **W:** Have you ever listened to the songs of _____?
   **M:** Have you ever been to the _____?
(5) **W:** How many _____ do you have every week?
   **M:** None. Our school has _____ any subject not directly related to the Entrance Exam.

## Task 2  Answering the Questions

*Directions: You will hear 5 recorded questions. Listen carefully and choose the proper answer to each question. The questions will be read twice.*

(1) A. The guitar          B. The violin
    C. The piano.          D. The trumpet
(2) A. Rock and roll       B. Classical music
    C. Country music       D. Folk music
(3) A. Yes, he does.       B. No, he doesn't.
    C. Yes, because he is a good Disco dancer.
    D. No, he is anything but a music lover.
(4) A. With a slow beat    B. Lively
    C. Melodious           D. Loud
(5) A. Doing her homework  B. Cooking
    C. Feeding her baby
    D. Talking with her friends

### Task 3  Oral Practice

*Warm-Up 1: Match the expressions in the left column with the expressions in the right column so as to form 7 short dialogues.*

| | |
|---|---|
| (1) —Do you know that Whitney Houston died 2 days ago? | —I thought it was great! Madonna is my favorite pop star. |
| (2) —When shall we go to the concert? | —Since I was 5 years old. |
| (3) —What do you know about Mozart? | —Yeah, it's a very heart-moving song. |
| (4) —Which do you like better, pop music or folk music? | —Really? It's very sorrowful news. She's a great singer. |
| (5) —How do you like the rock concert? | —It begins at 7 p.m.. We can leave at 6:30. |
| (6) —How long have you been learning to play the piano? | —I prefer folk music. |
| (7) —Have you ever heard *I Will Always Love You*? | —He is a master in classical music. |

*Warm-Up 2: Work with your partner to practise the following useful expressions.*
(1) Why do you like pop music/classical music/folk music/rock and roll...?
(2) Can you play the piano/violin/flute/guitar/drum/two-stringed fiddle...?
(3) I think classical music is stress-relieving/rock-and-roll is exciting/country music is peaceful...
(4) Will you go to the concert/theatre/ball... with me?
(5) Who's your favorite pop singer?
(6) Music can make you happy when you are sad/refreshed when you are tired/heartened when you are depressed.
(7) Music teaches us a lot as books do.

**Dialogue**

*A is a Chinese student. B is an American student. They are talking about music.*

A: Do you like music?
B: Yeah! Classical, Pop, Ambient, and light tunes... I like them all.
A: Music makes me happy, especially when I'm in a bad mood.
B: I also like Chinese music. Could you tell me the names of some good pieces?
A: Why don't you try listening to the *Reflection of the Moon on Spring (Er Quan Ying Yue)* and *the Butterfly Lovers (Liang Shanbo yu Zhu Yingtai)*. The first is a fiddle solo and the second is a violin concerto; they are two famous pieces of Chinese music.

B: Do you have them? Could I borrow them for a while?

A: Of course you can. I'll take the CD with them on it to you tomorrow.

### New Words and Expressions

| | | | |
|---|---|---|---|
| tune | /tju:n/ | n. | 曲调,调子 |
| mood | /mu:d/ | n. | 心情,情绪 |
| reflection | /rɪˈflɛkʃ(ə)n/ | n. | 倒影,反射 |
| spring | /sprɪŋ/ | n. | 春天,弹簧,泉水 |
| fiddle | /ˈfɪd(ə)l/ | n. | 小提琴 |
| solo | /ˈsəʊləʊ/ | n. | 独奏,独唱 |
| concerto | /kənˈtʃəːtəʊ, -ˈtʃɛːtəʊ/ | n. | 协奏曲 |

**Task 4  Role Play**

(1) Your friend is asking you about the concert you attended last night. Make up a dialogue. The expressions given below may be of some help to you.

### Expressions

| | | | |
|---|---|---|---|
| performance | /pəˈfɔːm(ə)ns/ | n. | 表演,表现 |
| superstar | /ˈsuːpəstɑː, ˈsjuː-/ | n. | 天王巨星 |
| be known to all | | | 家喻户晓 |
| audience | /ˈɔːdɪəns/ | n. | 听众,观众,读者 |
| be reluctant to | | | 不情愿,不愿意 |

(2) You are talking with a friend about a song which has an enormous impact on you. Make up a dialogue. The expressions given below may be of some help to you.

### Expressions

| | | | |
|---|---|---|---|
| beat | /biːt/ | n. | 节奏,拍子 |
| melodious | /mɪˈləʊdɪəs/ | adj. | 旋律优美的 |
| lyrics | /ˈlɪrɪks/ | n. | 歌词 |
| encourage | /ɪnˈkʌrɪdʒ, ɛn-/ | v. | 鼓励,促进 |
| struggle for | | | 为……努力 |

### Task 5　Leisure Time: Learning to Sing a Song

1. Listen to the song "I Will Always Love You".
2. Listen to the song again and fill in the missing words.

If I should stay, I would only be in your way. So I go, but I know I think of you every _____ of the way. And I will always love you! I will always love you! You, my darling you! Bitter _____ memories, that is all I'm taking with me. So, goodbye. Please don't cry. We both know I'm not what you need. And I will always love you! I will always love you! I hope life _____ you kind.

And I hope you have all you've _____ of. And I wish to you _____ and happiness. But above all this I wish you love. And I will always love you! I will always love you! I will always love you! I will always love you! I will always love you! I will always love you! You, darling, I love you! Ooh, I always, I always love you!

3. Learn to sing the song after the singer.

## Part III　Reading

*Text A*

### How Adele Conquered the World

Adele came to the Grammy Awards ceremony with six nominations and finally won six awards. Her song "Rolling in the Deep" is made Song of the Year, and the top selling album of 2011, "21", is made album of the year.

Adele Laurie Blue Adkins, better known as Adele, was born on May 5th, 1988. She is a British recording artist and songwriter. Her hometown was in Tottenham in north London, UK. She lived with her single mother named Penny. Adele's father separated from Adele's mother when Adele was 3 years, which Adele has not forgiven.

She began singing at age four and tells that she became crazy about voices. Adele has cited the Spice Girls as a major influence on her love and passion for music, stating that "they made me what I am today".

Adele's first album is of the soul genre, with lyrics describing heartbreak and relationship. "19", named for her age at the time she started recording it, entered the British charts at number one. The song "Chasing Pavements" reached number two on the UK Chart, and stayed there for four weeks.

By the beginning of 2009, listeners and critics started to describe Adele as unique. All Music wrote that "Adele is simply too magical to compare her to anyone". Adele released her second studio album, 21, on 24

January 2011 in the UK and 22 February in the US. The album's sound is described as classic and country music.

Following throat surgery in November, Adele made her live comeback at the 2012 Grammy Awards on 12 February. Adele said that her album 21 was inspired by her ex-boyfriend and the heartbreak. "This record is inspired by something that is really normal and everyone's been through it—a rubbish relationship".

Still, this just adds to the Adele's story—an ordinary girl genuinely living in the kind of "dream". It is perhaps this unexpected nature to her success that makes it sweetest of all.

### New Words

| | | | |
|---|---|---|---|
| ceremony | /ˈsɛrɪməni/ | n. | 典礼 |
| ☆nomination | /nɒmɪˈneɪʃ(ə)n/ | n. | 提名 |
| award | /əˈwɔːd/ | n. | 奖 |
| album | /ˈælbəm/ | n. | 音乐专辑 |
| recording | /rɪˈkɔːdɪŋ/ | n. | 唱片 |
| ★separate | /ˈsɛp(ə)rət/ | v. | 分开 |
| ☆crazy | /ˈkreɪzi/ | adj. | 对……着迷 |
| state | /steɪt/ | v. | 叙述 |
| describe | /dɪˈskrʌɪb/ | v. | 描述 |
| chart | /tʃɑːt/ | n. | 唱片的每周流行榜 |
| critic | /ˈkrɪtɪk/ | n. | 评论家 |
| ★magical | /ˈmadʒɪk(ə)l/ | adj. | 不可思议的 |
| ★surgery | /ˈsəːdʒ(ə)ri/ | n. | 外科手术 |
| comeback | /ˈkʌmbak/ | n. | 恢复 |
| inspire | /ɪnˈspʌɪə/ | v. | 赋……以灵感,给……启发 |
| rubbish | /ˈrʌbɪʃ/ | n. | 毫无价值的 |
| ☆genuinely | /ˈdʒɛnjʊɪnli/ | adv. | 真诚地 |
| unexpected | /ʌnɪkˈspɛktɪd, ʌnɛk-/ | adj. | 意想不到的 |

## Phrases and Expressions

| | |
|---|---|
| known as | 作为……而闻名 |
| forgive ... for | 原谅…… |
| be crazy about | 对……狂热 |
| soul genre | 灵歌类型 |
| compare ... to... | 比作 |
| be inspired by | 受……启发 |

## Proper Names

| | |
|---|---|
| Adele | 阿黛尔 |
| Grammy Awards | 格莱美奖 |
| Tottenham | 托特纳姆 |
| Spice Girls | 英国辣妹组合 |
| All Music | 音乐数据库 |

## Exercises

Directions: Answer the following questions according to the passage.

1. How many awards has Adele won at the Grammy Awards Ceremony?
2. Did Adele enjoy her family life as a child?
3. Which music group helped develop Adele's music style?
4. What did Adele mean by "they made me what I am today"?
5. What do Adele's fans think of her?
6. When did her second album come out? How successful was it?
7. What mainly influenced her album 21?
8. Did she have a difficult time getting through her unsuccessful love with her ex-boyfriend?

Directions: Choose the best meaning of each italicized word according to the context and try to tell how you get the answer.

1. And the top selling album of 2011, "21", is made *album* of the year.
   A. 影集   B. 邮册   C. 音乐专辑

2. Adele's father *separated from her mother when* Adele was 3 years, which Adele has not forgiven.
   A. 独立的   B. 离开   C. 隔离

3. She began singing at age four and asserts that she became *crazy about* voices.
   A. 受……困扰的   B. 对……痴迷的
   C. 对……发疯的

4. 19, named for her age at the time she started recording it, entered the British *charts* at number one.
   A. 图表   B. 海图   C. 排行榜

34

5. This record is inspired by something that is really normal and everyone's been through it—a *rubbish* relationship.
   A. 垃圾    B. 质量差的    C. 一文不值的

## Vocabulary

*Directions: Match each word in column A with its definition in Column B*

| Column A | Column B |
|---|---|
| 1. ceremony | a. sincerely, really |
| 2. conquer | b. be attracted by |
| 3. award | c. an important social or religious event |
| 4. separate | d. one's body cut open to repair or remove |
| 5. magical | e. to get control of |
| 6. be crazy about | f. a prize or money given to someone for what they've done |
| 7. come back | g. stop living together |
| 8. genuinely | h. used to describe something that is surprising |
| 9. unexpected | i. difficult to understand |
| 10. surgery | j. to return; to become popular or fashionable again |

*Directions: Complete the following sentences with words from Column A above. Change the forms where necessary.*

1. Research suggests that children whose parents _____ are more likely to drop out of high school.
2. The boy seemed to _____ animals.
3. Never change your appointment unless something _____ happens.
4. It is known that The Normans _____ England in 1066.
5. Liu Qian's performance is so _____ that the audiences are quite confused.
6. She required a _____ on her right knee as soon as possible.
7. A lot of young girls are on a diet because they _____ worry about their weight.
8. Who'd have thought that hippy gear would ever _____ ?
9. Many sports fans are looking forward to the opening _____ of 30th Olympic Games in London.
10. Rose was greatly honored when she received her _____ as the outstanding manager of the year.

*Directions: Translate the following sentences into English..*

1. In America, parents _____ (被邀请参加孩子们的毕业典礼).
2. (美国人对速度的崇尚)_____ has urged the food business.
3. I can (原谅你的错误)_____, but I can't forgive your dishonesty.
4. It is Dr. Smith _____ (邀请来给我们作报告的人史密斯博士)
5. Samuel Longhorn Clemens, _____ _____ (以马克·吐温更出名), is one of

America's famous writers.

6. Can you _____ (描述一下那个失踪男孩的相貌)?

**Text B**

## Whitney Houston, "We Will Always Love You"

Whitney Houston, who ruled as pop music's queen until her royal voice and brilliant image were damaged by drug use, strange behavior and a noisy marriage to singer Bobby Brown, died Saturday. She was 48.

Houston was pronounced dead at 3:55 p.m. in her room on the fourth floor of the hotel. Her body remained there and Beverly Hills detectives were investigating. Houston was found "underwater and unconscious" in the bathtub, according to Beverly Hills police.

What is the cause? In the circumstances of her death, and Houston's history of drug use, many have speculated that the singer died after taking a mix of drugs and alcohol.

Houston is a very talented singer, and she also pursued modeling and acting. She was born on August 9, 1963 in New Jersey. By age 11, Houston was performing at her Baptist church and began accompanying her mother in concert.

She is inarguably one of the biggest female pop stars of all time. Houston's amazing technique of singing is outstanding over nearly every soul singer—male or female and drew many imitators. Her achievements are quite unusual. Just to name a few, she became the first artist ever to have seven continuous songs hitting number one, and "I Will Always Love You" became nothing less than the biggest hit single in rock history.

It is a pity that Houston's death came on the eve of music's biggest night—the Grammy Awards. It's a stage where she once ruled, and her death was sure a shocking event on Sunday's ceremony.

Houston was supposed to appear at the gala, and it was told by Associated Press that she would perhaps perform: "It's her favorite night of the year ... (so) who knows by the end of the evening..." he said. Producer Jimmy Jam, who had worked with Houston, said he expected the evening would become a gift to her.

## Unit 2  Pop Music

### New Words

| | | | |
|---|---|---|---|
| rule | /ruːl/ | v. | 统治 |
| ★royal | /ˈrɔɪəl/ | adj. | 高贵的 |
| brilliant | /ˈbrɪlj(ə)nt/ | adj. | 辉煌的 |
| drug | /drʌg/ | n. | 毒品 |
| pronounce | /prəˈnaʊns/ | v. | 宣布 |
| ★investigate | /ɪnˈvɛstɪgeɪt/ | v. | 调查 |
| unconscious | /ʌnˈkɒnʃəs/ | adj. | 失去知觉的 |
| ★circumstance | /ˈsɜːkəmst(ə)ns/ | v. | 环境 |
| ☆speculate | /ˈspɛkjʊleɪt/ | v. | 推断 |
| talented | /ˈtaləntɪd/ | adj. | 有才干的 |
| perform | /pəˈfɔːm/ | v. | 表演 |
| ★accompany | /əˈkʌmpəni/ | v. | 陪同 |
| unusual | /ʌnˈjuːʒʊəl/ | adj. | 罕有的, 独特的 |
| continuous | /kənˈtɪnjʊəs/ | adj. | 连续的, |
| ★shock | /ʃɒk/ | v. | 震惊 |
| gala | /ˈgɑːlə, ˈgeɪlə/ | n. | 盛会 |

### Phrases and Expressions

| | |
|---|---|
| pop music | 流行音乐 |
| according to | （表示依据）根据, 按照 |
| nothing less than | 完全 |

### Proper Names

| | | | |
|---|---|---|---|
| Whitney Houston | | | 惠特尼·休斯顿 |
| Bobby Brown | | | 鲍比·布朗 |
| Beverly Hills | | | 比弗利山庄 |
| Baptist | /ˈbaptɪst/ | n. | 浸礼会 |
| Associated Press | | | （美）联合通讯社（简称美联社） |

# Exercises

*Directions: Decide whether the following statements are true (T) or false (F) according to the information in the passage.*

1. Whitney Houston was addicted to drug use. ( )
2. Whitney Houston died unexpectedly, which was a shocking event in the music world. ( )
3. Houston refused to appear at the gala on the eve of music's biggest night. ( )
4. Her technique of singing is so outstanding that many singers imitate her music style. ( )
5. Houston's musical talent was shown as early as in her teenage. ( )
6. According to detectives, Houston died from heart attack. ( )

*Directions: Guess the meanings of the words and phrases in the box according to the passage. Then, use them to complete the following sentences, changing the form if necessary.*

| nothing less than | anticipate | perform | accompany |
| unusual | according to | speculate | |

1. His wife _____ him on the trip.
2. It was _____ a disaster.
3. _____ Mike, it's a great movie.
4. We all _____ about the reason for her absence.
5. A computer can _____ many tasks at once.
6. She was a truly _____ woman.
7. We eagerly _____ the day we would leave school.

*Directions: Pay attention to different parts of speech and select the appropriate word to fill in the blanks.*

1. conscious   consciously   consciousness
    a. I can't remember any more — I must have lost _____.
    b. Whether _____ or unconsciously, you made a choice.
    c. She's very _____ of the problems involved.
2. argue   argument   arguable   arguably
    a. It is _____ whether parents should pay their children for the housework they have done.
    b. He is _____ the best actor of his generation.
    c. My brothers are always _____.
    d. We had an _____ with the waiter about the bill.

3. investigate   investigation   investigative   investigator
   a. "What was that noise?" "I'll go and _____."
   b. She is still under _____.
   c. The article was an excellent piece of _____ journalism.
   d. He worked as a private _____.
4. speculate   speculator   speculation   speculative
   a. He is a property _____.
   b. The report is highly _____ and should be ignored.
   c. Our _____ proved right.
   d. It's useless to _____ why he did it.

Directions: *First translate the following English sentences into Chinese. Then, pay attention to the italicized parts in the English sentences and translate the Chinese sentences by simulating the structure of the English sentences.*

1. Houston was found underwater and unconscious in the bathtub, *according to* Beverly Hills police.
   根据我们的记录，你已经缺席六次了。
2. *It was told by* the Associated Press that she would perhaps perform a song.
   据他同事说，汤姆下周要去北京出差。
3. *By* age 11, Houston was performing at her Baptist church and began accompanying her mother in concert.
   下星期的这个时候我们将在纽约。
4. *It's a pity* that Houston's death came *on the eve of* music's biggest night — the Grammy Awards.
   真是遗憾，迈克在选举前夕病倒了。
5. It's a stage *where* she once ruled, and her death was sure a shocking event on Sunday's ceremony.
   这是为数不多的几个靠左行驶的国家之一。

Directions: *Group activity.*
Discussing the following questions:
1. What is success or failure for a pop star? What is the trouble for some famous people?
2. What are the best attitudes, in your opinion, towards success or failure?

## Part IV  Grammar

### 句子结构

英语句子分为简单句和复合句。所谓的简单句,就是只包含一个主谓结构的句子。复合句又分成并列句和复杂句。

**1. 简单句**

简单句,即只有一个主谓结构的句子。除了特殊情况,英语句子中都有主语、谓语(或表语),有时候还有宾语;而且除了倒装句等特殊句型,一般情况下,主语、谓语、宾语的先后顺序是固定的。根据动词的特性,将英语句子分为五个基本句型:

> 1)主语 + 系动词 + 表语
> 2)主语 + 不及物动词(+ 其他成分)
> 3)主语 + 及物动词 + 宾语
> 4)主语 + 及物动词 + 双宾语
> 5)主语 + 及物动词 + 宾语 + 宾语补足语

我们在学习5个基本句型时,主要关心每个句型中的出题点在哪里。

(一)第一句型:主语 + 系动词 + 表语

　　常见的系动词有:look, feel, sound, smell, taste, get, become, come, go, turn, grow, keep, seem 等。

You look pale. Do you feel unwell? 你脸色苍白,感到不舒服吗?
Our dream will come true. 我们的梦想即将实现。

(二)第二句型:主语 + 不及物动词 (+ 其他成分)

| 不及物动词 | 及物动词 |
| --- | --- |
| rise /rose / risen (升起) | raise /raised / raised (提高) |
| arise / arose / arisen (from) (产生) | arouse / aroused / aroused (唤起) |
| lie / lay / lain (躺下) | lay / laid / laid (放下) |
| arrive (到达) | reach (到达) |
| wait (等待) | await (等待) |

Everybody laughed. 大家都笑了。
I live in Beijing. 我住在北京。

(三)第三句型:主语 + 及物动词 + 宾语

I like English very much. 我非常喜欢英语。

I forgot to close the windows when I left home yesterday.
昨天外出的时候我忘记关窗户了。
This waiting room needs cleaning. 候车室需要打扫。

(四) 第四句型：主语 + 及物动词 + 双宾语

有些动词（主要是"授予动词"）后面需要或可以接双宾语结构，如：give, write, buy, send, make 等。

You may send him an E-mail or write him a letter.
你可以发电子邮件给他或者写信给他。

这个句子也可使用以下结构：

You may send an E-mail (to him) or write a letter to him. （"to"和"for"是连接双宾语结构的重要介词）

We have to inform the family of the patient's condition as soon as possible.
我们得尽快将病人的病情通知其家属。

Have the family been informed of the patient's condition?
已经将病人的病情通知其家人了吗？

(五) 第五句型：主语 + 及物动词 + 宾语 + 宾语补足语

The director wants you to come right now. 主任要你马上就来。
His joke made us laughing for a couple of minutes.
他的笑话让我们笑了好几分钟。
I am going to have (get) my watch repaired. 我去修一下表。

注：make, let, have 等使役动词，see, hear, notice, observe, watch, look at, listen to 等感觉动词后面接宾语补足语的不定式要省略 to：

Shall I have him come here? 要我叫他来吗？
I won't have him cheat me. 我决不容许他欺骗我。（否定式，表示"容许"）

上述句型变为被动语态时，一般要加 "to"，如：

The nurse made the patient eat something. 护士让病人吃了点东西。
→The patient was made to eat something.

## 2. 并列句

并列句就是两个或两个以上的简单句，由表示并列关系的连词或标点符号连接而成。常见的连词：and, not only...but also, neither...nor..., or, either...or..., otherwise, but, yet, while, so, for 等。阅读中遇到并列关系的句子，一般情况下是以连词为界限，将句子分成前、后几个部分，并分别来分析，各句的意思一般可以单独理解，最后将各句合并即可。

I hate grammar while he loves it. (以 while 为界，可分为前后两个小句子)
我讨厌语法，而他却很喜欢语法。

The watch was cheap, but it goes quite well. 这块表虽然便宜，但走得很准。
I was ill that day, otherwise I would have taken part in the sports meet.

那天我病了,否则我会去参加运动会的。

### 3. 主从复合句

主从复合句即复杂句,也是由两个或两个以上的句子构成。根据其在句中的用法,可以分为以下三类从句:名词性从句,形容词性从句和副词性从句。

名词性从句:主语从句,宾语从句,表语从句,同位语从句

形容词性从句(定语从句):限制性,非限制性

副词性从句(状语从句):时间,地点,原因,条件,目的,让步,方式,结果

The sad thing is that the ugly man with a lot of money chooses living alone. (表语)

What the ugly man chooses is living alone.(主语)

We all know that the ugly man chooses living alone.(宾语)

The thing that the ugly man with a lot of money chooses living alone was known to everyone. (同位语)

The ugly man who has a lot of money chooses living alone.(定语)

Although the ugly man has a lot of money, he chooses living alone.(状语)

## Exercises

*Directions: Are they simple sentences, compound sentences or complex sentences? (判断下列句子是简单句、并列句还是复合句).*

1. We often study Chinese history on Friday afternoon.
2. The boy who offered me his seat is called Tom.
3. There is a chair in this room, isn't there?
4. My brother and I go to school at half past seven in the morning and come back home at seven in the evening.
5. He is in Class One and I am in Class Two.
6. He was fond of drawing when he was yet a child.
7. Neither has he changed his mind, nor will he do so.
8. What he said at the meeting is very important, isn't it?
9. The farmer is showing the boy how to plant a tree.
10. Both Tom and Jack enjoy country music.

## Part V  Applied Writing

### Greeting Cards (贺卡)

贺卡是人们在遇到喜庆的日期或事件的时候互相表示问候的一种卡片,人们通常赠送

贺卡的日子包括生日、圣诞节、元旦、春节、母亲节、父亲节、情人节等节日。当前电子贺卡(E-card)以其快速便捷,节约环保的特点,迅速成为一种时尚。

　　贺卡一般由称呼、贺词、祝贺人签名三部分组成。称呼指送卡人对受贺人的称呼,一般写在卡片的左上方,称呼前可加也可不加"to",如:To Mr. Smith 或 Mr. Smith. 由于贺卡是沟通人与人之间的情感交往,而此种交往又往往以短句表达,言简意赅,贺语就出现了程式化。通常写一些固定的贺词用语,也可根据实际情况写一些简短的表示感谢和良好祝愿的话。祝贺人签名写在贺卡的右下方,姓名前加 from(也可不加),如:(From) your friend

【格式】

_____(称呼)

_____

_____

_____(贺词)

_____(签名)

Sample 1:

To Mr. Wu,

　　We all like having you as our friend. Thank you very much for teaching us so well.
　　Good luck with you!

From all your students

Basic Expressions（常用表达）

◆ Greetings

(1) For Christmas and the New Year:

☆Happy New Year (to you)/ Merry Christmas!
☆Wish you a happy New Year/ a Merry Christmas!
☆Best wishes for a happy New Year/ a Merry Christmas!

☆ Warm regards and season's greetings.

(2) For a birthday/ a wedding anniversary:

☆ Happy birthday(to you)!

☆ Many happy returns of your wedding anniversary!

(3) For Teachers' Day

☆ Happy Teachers' Day!

☆ Best wishes for a happy Teachers' Day!

☆ Thank you for your hard work/ help/ teaching us so well!

◆ Good Wishes

(1) To someone in hospital:

☆ Best wishes for a speedy recovery.

☆ Get well soon!

☆ Warmest Get-Well Wishes.

(2) For an examination/ an interview for a job:

☆ Good luck in your examination/ interview!

◆ Congratulations

(1) On success in doing something:

☆ Hearty congratulations on your success!

(2) On a marriage:

☆ Hearty congratulations on your marriage and best wishes to you both!

☆ Best wishes for a long and happy married life to you both.

◆ 其他

☆ Good luck for your future! 祝你今后一切顺利！

☆ Good luck with you! 好运伴你！

☆ I wish you a happy life! 祝你生活幸福！

☆ Wishing you many future successes! 祝你今后获得更大成就！

☆ I want to wish you longevity and health! 愿您健康长寿！

## Exercises

*Directions: This part is to test your ability to do practical writing. You are required to write:*

1. A New Year Card for Uncle Tony, from Sam.
2. A Christmas Card for Mr. and Mrs. King, from Kate
3. A Teachers' Day Card for your English teacher.
4. A Birthday Card for your classmate Peter, from Jim.

## Part VI  Cultural Express

### Bruno Mars: Just the Way You Are

Bruno Mars was born and raised in Honolulu (火奴鲁鲁), Hawaii. His parents are of Puerto Rican (波多黎各) and Filipino (菲律宾) descent. He was given the nickname 'Bruno' as a child, after the wrestler Bruno Sammartino. Bruno Mars is an American singer-songwriter and music producer, perhaps best known for co-writing "Nothing on you" by B.o.B.

Mars was one of six children and his family was a musical one, and he was a music fan since he was just a kid. From a young age, he was impersonating and performing songs by influential artists such as Michael Jackson (迈克尔·杰克逊) and Elvis Presley (猫王). He was even named Little Elvis in Mid Week magazine and once played the younger version of the late singer in 1992 movie "Honeymoon in Vegas" (维加斯蜜月). After graduating from President Theodore Roosevelt High School, he moved to Los Angeles to pursue a musical career.

Despite having experience of acting in front of camera, Hernandez decided to pursue career in music. Better known with stage name Bruno Mars, he wrote many hit singles for other artists before laying vocals for his own track. He helped Flo Rida to write "Right Round" and "Waving Flag" with K'naan together.

Bruno Mars' debut album, entitled "Doo-Wops & Hooligans", was released in October 2010. The lead single, "Just the Way You Are" performed well in the US charts and climbed to No. 9 on Billboard Hot (美国音乐排行榜) 100. The album was preceded with an extended play "It's Better If You Don't Understand" which came out in May in the same year.

In addition, he served as featured guests in B.o.B's "Nothing on You" and Travis McCoy's "Billionaire". Both songs successfully brought his two pals to stardom and introduced himself as a solo recording artist. Enough with working for other musicians, he decided to work on his own record.

Mar's music has been noted for displaying a wide variety of styles and influences, including pop, rock, reggae, R&B, soul, and hip hop. In addition, Mars states that growing up in Hawaii influenced his music, giving the songs a reggae sound. He explains that "In Hawaii some of the biggest radio stations are reggae. The local bands are heavily influenced by Bob Marley. That music brings people together. It's not urban music or pop music. It's just songs. That's what makes it cross over so well. The song comes first".

Lyrically, many of Mars' songs have been described as "feel-good", carefree, and optimistic; however, darker subjects are shown in songs. His co-producer Philip Lawrence says, "What people don't know is there's a darker part in Bruno Mars". The songs such as "Grenade", "Liquor Store Blues", and "Talking to the Moon" detail failed relationships and self-destructive behavior.

(Source: http://www.contactmusic.com/info/bruno_mas)

## 拓展词汇

**音乐种类**

blues 蓝调；rock & roll 摇滚；hip-hop 嘻哈；rap 说唱；jazz 爵士；electronic music 电子音乐；Latin music 拉丁音乐；country music 乡村音乐；folk 现代民歌；light music 轻音乐

**格莱美奖项**

Album of the Year 年度最佳专辑；Record of the Year 年度最佳唱片

**音乐元素**

pitch 音高；rhythm 节奏；dynamics 力度；timbre 音色；texture 谐和；scale 音阶；idiom 音调

### 民族乐器
flute 笛子；urheen 二胡；pipa 琵琶；huqin 胡琴；drum 鼓

### 西洋乐器
saxophone 萨克斯；violin 小提琴；viola 中提琴；cello 大提琴；harp 竖琴；bass 贝司；guitar 吉他 piano 钢琴；electronic keyboard 电子琴

### 音乐符号
staff 五线谱；clef 谱号；treble clef 高音谱号；bass clef 低音谱号；key signature 音调符号；quarter tone 四分音；time signature 拍子记号

### 西方乐曲种类
symphony 交响曲；symphonic poem 交响诗；concerto 协奏曲；overture 序曲；serenade 小夜曲；march 进行曲；sonata 奏鸣曲；fantasia 幻想曲；etude 练习曲；rhapsody 狂想曲

### 音乐剧
comedy 喜剧；script 剧本；opera house 歌剧院；broadway 百老汇；ballet 芭蕾舞

# Unit 3

# Sports

*Learning Objectives:*

You are able to:

☞ Identify some basic sounds of letters

☞ Use the proper expressions to comment on sports

☞ Know the use of nouns & pronouns

☞ Write Lost and Found

You are suggested to:

☞ Be familiar with some sports culture

# Unit 3  Sports

Sport is all forms of competitive physical activity which, through casual or organized participation, aims to use, maintain or improve physical fitness and provide entertainment to participants. Hundreds of sports exist, from those requiring only two participants to those with hundreds of simultaneous participants, either in teams or competing as individuals. Sports are usually governed by a set of rules or customs, which serve to ensure fair competition. Winning can be determined by physical events such as scoring goals or crossing a line first, or by the determination of judges who are scoring elements of the sporting performance.

## Part I  Phonetics

### Task 1  Identifying Their Pronunciations

*Directions: Listen to the following words and read after the speaker, paying attention to the colored parts.*

| /ʌ/ | /ɑː/ | /eɪ/ | /aɪ/ | /ɔɪ/ |
| /ʃ/ | /ʒ/ | /θ/ | /ð/ | /h/ |

| | | | | |
|---|---|---|---|---|
| (1) bus | cup | under | us | mum |
| (2) afternoon | class | dark | car | ask |
| (3) make | eight | grey | rain | play |
| (4) like | my | minus | bye | right |
| (5) oil | boy | noise | moisture | poison |
| (6) bush | ship | shot | shop | fish |
| (7) measure | usually | occasion | vision | leisure |
| (8) thing | three | mouth | thick | throw |
| (9) with | their | this | other | brother |
| (10) who | whose | how | house | hot |

49

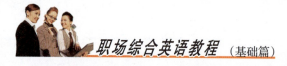

Practice: Write down the sound of the underlined part of the words.

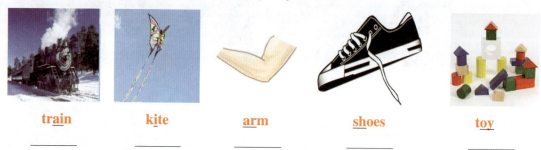

| tr<u>ai</u>n | k<u>i</u>te | <u>a</u>rm | <u>sh</u>oes | t<u>oy</u> |

_____   _____   _____   _____   _____

## Task 2    Appreciating a Poem

*Directions: Listen to the poem written by Emily Dickinson "If Recollecting Were Forgetting". Choose the words you hear to fill in the blanks.*

| recollect | /ˌrɛkəˈlɛkt/ | v. | 记起,想起 |
| merry | /ˈmɛri/ | adj. | 欢乐的,愉快的 |
| mourn | /mɔːn/ | v. | 哀悼,为……哀痛 |
| gay | /geɪ/ | adj. | 快乐的,欢快的,轻松的 |
| blithe | /blʌɪð/ | adj. | 欢乐的,愉快的 |
| gather | /ˈgaðə/ | v. | (使)聚集,集合 |

---

**Poem          If Recollecting were Forgetting**

*Emily Dickinson*

If recollecting _____ (war, were) forgetting,
Then I remember _____ (lot, not).
And if forgetting, recollecting,
How near I had _____ (forgot, frog).
And if to _____ (ms, miss), were merry,
And to mourn, were gay,
How _____ (very, vary) blithe the fingers.
That gathered _____ (this, these), Today!

---

## Task 3    Time for Fun: Tongue Twister

*Directions: Practise the tongue twister sentence by sentence after the speaker. Pay attention to the sounds.*

(1) Nine nice night nurses are nursing nicely.
(2) A snow-white swan swam swiftly to catch a slowly swimming snake in a lake.
(3) I wish to wish the wish you wish to wish, but if you wish the wish the witch wishes, I won't wish the wish you wish to wish.

● Unit 3   Sports ●

## Part II   Listening and Speaking

### Task 1   Short Dialogues

*Directions: Listen to the following short dialogues and fill in the blanks with the information you get from the recording. Each dialogue will be read twice.*

(1) **W:** Is Taiji _____ in your country?
   **M:** Yes. I find the _____ very nice.
(2) **W:** These days the National Games are the _____ TV shows.
   **M:** Yes. I watched many games like gymnastics and _____.
(3) **M:** What _____ do you like?
   **W:** I like playing table tennis, _____ and jogging in the morning.
(4) **M:** Do you think sports are good to our _____ _____?
   **W:** Sure. Playing sports can make us _____, quicker and happier.
(5) **M:** Do you know Messi has been _____ FIFA world player recently?
   **W:** Yes, of course. He is definitely a _____ football player.

### Task 2   Answering the Questions

*Directions: You will hear 5 recorded questions. Listen carefully and choose the proper answer to each question. The questions will be read twice.*

(1) A. In London        B. In Sydney
    C. In Athens        D. In Beijing
(2) A. Soccer           B. Golf
    C. Basketball       D. Tennis
(3) A. Ballet           B. Qigong
    C. Judo             D. Karate
(4) A. Back stroke      B. Free style
    C. Crawl            D. Breast stroke
(5) A. Arsenal vs. Manchester
    B. New Castle vs. Manchester
    C. Arsenal vs. Liverpool
    D. Everton vs. Fulham

## Task 3　Oral Practice

*Warm-Up 1: Match the expressions in the left column with the expressions in the right column so as to form 7 short dialogues.*

(1) —Who's your favorite soccer star?　　　　—It's very tight.
(2) —Do you like to go rock climbing with us?　　—I like Cristiano Ronaldo best.
(3) —How is the match going?　　　　　　—You are really sporty.
(4) —Do you do aerobics every morning in the park?　—But I think enough sleep is more important for our health.
(5) —You should get up early to do some morning exercises every day.　—No, but I do shadow-boxing instead.
(6) —You won. Congratulations!　　　—Thank you. It's a narrow victory.
(7) —I want to learn to play golf.　　—Great! It's my favorite sport.

*Warm-Up 2: Work with your partner to practise the following useful expressions.*

(1) What's your favorite sport?
(2) Do you like playing football/volleyball/tennis/badminton/basketball/golf...?
(3) Adequate physical exercises are very important for our health.
(4) Terrific! Our national team won the game.
(5) Friendship is the first, competition the second.
(6) The spirit of the Olympics is *higher, faster and mightier*.
(7) Would you like to come over to play chess with me if you are free?

**Dialogue**

A: Hi. What's wrong with you? Your face is very pale.
B: You know the Australian Open is going on and I am busy with it. So...
A: Oh, I forget it. You are a tennis fan. Who interests you?
B: Certainly Roger Federer. He is my idol. And who is your idol?
A: Kobe Bryant. I like NBA best. He is the best player.
B: Yeah, so he is. I also like him. He is a player full of wisdom.
A: In China, he owns the most fans. Roger is also excellent.
B: He has owned the most Grand Slams.

A: He had twin daughters a few months ago and became a father.
B: Yes. He lives happily so I'm very happy.
A: Good luck for Roger. And take care of yourself.
B: Thank you.

### New Words and Expressions

| | | | |
|---|---|---|---|
| Australian Open | | | 澳大利亚网球公开赛 |
| fan | /fæn/ | n. | 迷,狂热爱好者 |
| idol | /ˈʌɪd(ə)l/ | n. | 偶像 |
| NBA | | | 美国职业篮球联赛 |
| wisdom | /ˈwɪzdəm/ | n. | 智慧,才智 |
| Grand Slam | | | (棒球)大满贯 |

**Task 4　Role Play**

(1) You and your friend are talking about the men's 100m final which is about to begin. Make up a dialogue. The expressions given below may be of some help to you.

### Expressions

| | | | |
|---|---|---|---|
| final | /ˈfʌɪn(ə)l/ | n. | 决赛,期终考试 |
| tense | /tɛns/ | adj. | 紧张的,绷紧的 |
| take the lead | | | 领先 |
| accelerate | /əkˈsɛləreɪt/ | v. | 加速,提前 |
| catch at | | | 抓住,赶上 |
| neck and neck | | | 并驾齐驱 |
| draw... away | | | 把……甩在后面 |
| hit the line | | | 撞线 |
| national banner | | | 国旗 |

(2) You and your friend are talking about how to keep fit. Make up a dialogue. The expressions given below may be of some help to you.

## Expressions

| | | | |
|---|---|---|---|
| keep fit | | | 保持健康 |
| diet | /ˈdʌɪət/ | n. | 日常饮食 |
| sound sleep | | | 良好的睡眠 |
| stay in a good mood | | | 保持好心情 |
| sense of humor | | | 幽默感 |
| proper exercise | | | 适量运动 |

**Task 5　Leisure Time: Learning to Sing a Song**

1. Listen to the song "Hand In Hand".
2. Listen to the song again and fill in the missing words.

### Hand In Hand

See the _____ in the sky
We feel the beating of our hearts together
This is our time to rise above
We know the chance is here to live forever
For all time
Hand in hand we stand
all across the _____
We can make this world a better place in
which to live
Hand in hand we can

start to understand
Breaking down the _____ that come
between us for all time
A li la
Every time we give it all
We feel the flame eternally inside us
Lift our _____ up to the sky
The morning calm helps us to live in _____
For all time

3. Learn to sing the song after the singer.

# Part III  Reading

### Text A

## Why Olympians Must Seize the Moment
*Iwan Thomas*

An Olympics is an amazing place to be. You sit in the canteen and you could see a seven-foot Chinese girl who is the best volleyball player in the world, and opposite you'd have an American basketball player you might have watched on television.

## Unit 3  Sports

All of a sudden you are among athletes you look up to. When you get to an Olympic village, you try not to get too excited. You've got to remember why you are there—to compete.

At an Olympics, you haven't got your home comforts. You might be sharing with an athlete who snores—simple things like that—but you've got to keep your focus.

There are the external pressures from friends and family, but you've got to be selfish and switch your phone off, tell your mum and dad and your friends to leave you for two weeks. You've got to realize why you are there. You've trained all year for the Olympics and you've got that small window of opportunity to get everything right.

It was amazing to get a silver medal in Atlanta. The proudest moment for me was seeing my mum and dad on my lap of honor.

When you go to the Olympics, you're a perfectionist. The silver medal was great, but it wasn't gold. At the time I thought, "I'm 21, I've got loads of Olympics ahead." But as it happened I had a lot of injuries. My advice is to seize the moment. You've got to grasp that opportunity and savor the moment.

Now as I get older and look back on it, I'm really proud of my medal, of all my medals. I know how much blood, sweat and tears have gone into winning them.

Notes: Welsh runner Iwan Thomas won a silver medal for Great Britain in the 4 × 400 meters relay at the 1996 Atlanta Olympics.

### New Words

| | | | |
|---|---|---|---|
| amazing | /əˈmeɪzɪŋ/ | adj. | 令人惊异的 |
| canteen | /kænˈtiːn/ | n. | 小卖部, 食堂, 小饭馆 |
| ★ athlete | /ˈæθliːt/ | n. | 运动员, 体育家, 强壮的人 |
| snore | /snɔː/ | v. | 打呼噜, 打鼾 |
| ☆ external | /ɪkˈstəːn(ə)l, ɛk-/ | adj. | 外来的, 外国的, 表面上的 |
| ★ switch | /swɪtʃ/ | v. | 转换, 关闭电流 |
| ★ load | /ləʊd/ | n. | 负荷, 装载, 工作量 |
| savor | /ˈseɪvə/ | v. | 品尝, 欣赏 |

## Phrases and Expressions

| | |
|---|---|
| all of a sudden | 突然 |
| look up to | 尊重,敬仰(某人) |
| share with | 与……共用,分享 |
| switch off | 关上 |
| loads of | 许多 |
| grasp the opportunity | 抓住机会 |
| be proud of | 对……感到自豪 |

## Exercises

*Directions: Answer the following questions according to the passage.*

1. What is an Olympian occasion like?
2. If you get to an Olympic village as an athlete, what should you remember?
3. Does an athlete have to forget friends and family while at an Olympics? Why or why not?
4. The athletes competing in the Olympics are really selfish and only think of themselves?
5. All athletes competing in Olympic Games have no choice but to win the gold medal, don't they?
6. What did the author mean by "When you go to the Olympics, you are a perfectionist"?
7. What's the proudest moment for Iwan Thomas?
8. Did Iwan Thomas think the blood, sweat, and tears he had worthwhile?

*Directions: Choose the best meaning of each italicized word according to the context and try to tell how you get the answer.*

1. You sit in the canteen and you could see a seven-foot Chinese girl who is the best volleyball player in the world, and *opposite* you'd have an American basketball player you might have watched on television.
   A. 相反的   B. 在对面   C. 正面的
2. All of a sudden you are among athletes you *look up to*.
   A. 崇拜   B. 查找   C. 期待
3. You might be *sharing* with an athlete who snores.
   A. 分享   B. 共用   C. 合住
4. You've trained all year for the Olympics and you have got that small *window of opportunity* to get everything right.
   A. 机会的窗口   B. 时机
   C. 窗户里的机会
5. The *proudest* moment for me was seeing my mum and dad on my lap of honor.
   A. 自负的   B. 傲慢的   C. 自豪的

Unit 3   Sports

# Vocabulary

Directions: Match each word in column A with its definition in Column B

| Column A | Column B |
| --- | --- |
| 1. athlete | a. caring only about oneself |
| 2. amazing | b. to admire or respect someone |
| 3. selfish | c. to turn off |
| 4. opposite | d. someone who is not satisfied unless it is perfect |
| 5. snore | e. to fully enjoy the taste or the smell of something |
| 6. external | f. someone who competes in sports competitions |
| 7. switch off | g. so surprising that you can't believe it |
| 8. perfectionist | h. relating to the outside of something |
| 9. look up to | i. as different as possible from something else |
| 10. savor | j. to breathe in a noisy way while sleeping |

Directions: Complete the following sentences with words from Column A above. Change the forms where necessary.

1. She sipped her wine, _____ every drop.
2. I've always _____ Madame Curie for great achievements in scientific research.
3. It is well known that Liu Xiang is a very promising _____.
4. I had thought the medicine would make him sleep, but it had the _____ effect.
5. Never make friends with _____ people, who won't think anything of you.
6. This skin medicine is for _____ use only and can't be swallowed.
7. Many top athletes are _____ who drive themselves to excel.
8. I heard him _____ and knew he had fallen asleep.
9. It's _____ for foreigners to see some Chinese drivers using mobile phones.
10. Remember to _____ before you leave the laboratory.

Directions: Translate the following sentences into English.

1. _____(突然), it rained heavily during children's camping in the forest.
2. I had thought the medicine was effective on the sleep, _____(结果相反).
3. _____(回顾过去), I realized how free I was then.
4. The students _____(崇拜) this accomplished teacher.
5. The old man drove _____ (速度快得惊人).
6. Olympic Games is _____ (千载难逢的良机) for many athletes.

57

## Text B

### Martial Ethics

Chinese Wushu embodies a profound philosophy and a sense of human life and social values. It can display the oriental civilization. Generally speaking, it evaluates man's behavior with such conceptions as the good and the evil, justice and injustice, and honesty and dishonesty.

Martial ethics is an essential part of Chinese martial arts. The main points of the martial ethics are:

### Respect for Human Life

In ancient China, human beings were regarded as the most valuable treasure of nature. It was for protecting and maintaining human life that Wushu took birth.

### Emphasis on Moral Principles

Moral principles provide the basis for maintaining a stable relationship between man and man, and between man and society.

### Emphasis on Moral Conduct and Manners

While learning martial skills, one should also cultivate the fine qualities. A sense of justice, diligence, persistence, honesty and hard work are also encouraged.

### Respect for the Teacher and Care for Each Other

In learning Wushu, one should try hard to master everything that is taught. Both teacher and student should take care of each other and treasure the friendship between them.

### Modesty and Eagerness

Those who learn martial arts should keep improving their skills and learn from each other to improve and be united and cooperative with each other.

### Freedom from Personal Grudges

In learning Wushu, one aims at improving one's physical conditions. One should not bully the weak or the innocent.

### Persistence and Perseverance

The practice of martial arts is a hard task which takes time and requires hard efforts. Steadiness and persistence are required.

## Unit 3  Sports

### New Words

| | | | |
|---|---|---|---|
| ethics | /ˈɛθɪks/ | n. | 道德规范,伦理学 |
| ★philosophy | /fɪˈlɒsəfi/ | n. | 哲理,哲学体系,世界观,人生观 |
| oriental | /ɔːrɪˈɛnt(ə)l, ɒr-/ | adj. | 东方的,东方人的,东方文化的,优质的 |
| ★civilization | /ˌsɪvɪlaɪˈzeɪʃ(ə)n/ | n. | 文明,文化,修养 |
| ★evaluate | /ɪˈvaljʊeɪt/ | v. | 评价 |
| conception | /kənˈsɛpʃ(ə)n/ | n. | 观念,设想,构想 |
| maintain | /meɪnˈteɪn, mənˈteɪn/ | v. | 保持,维持,保养,坚持 |
| emphasis | /ˈɛmfəsɪs/ | n. | 强调,着重,(轮廓、图形等的)鲜明,突出,重读 |
| persistence | /pəˈsɪst(ə)ns/ | n. | 坚持不懈 |
| modesty | /ˈmɒdɪsti/ | n. | 谦虚,谦逊 |
| eagerness | /ˈiːɡənəs/ | n. | 渴望,热心,热切 |
| ☆grudge | /ɡrʌdʒ/ | n. | 怨恨,妒忌 |
| ☆bully | /ˈbʊli/ | v. | 恐吓,威逼 |
| innocent | /ˈɪnəs(ə)nt/ | adj. | 无辜的,清白的,天真无邪的,无知的 |
| perseverance | /ˌpɜːsɪˈvɪər(ə)ns/ | n. | 坚持不懈,不屈不挠 |

### Phrases and Expressions

| | |
|---|---|
| respect for | 尊重 |
| take birth | 产生 |
| martial arts | 武术 |
| aim at | 力求达到,力争做到 |
| respect for human life | 尊重生命、以人为本 |
| emphasis on moral principles | 中华武德牢记心中 |
| emphasis on moral conduct and manners | 习武重视身心双修 |
| respect for the teacher and care for each other | 尊重师长、关爱他人 |
| modesty and eagerness | 谦虚好学、戒骄戒躁 |
| freedom from personal grudges | 心存善念、申张正义 |
| persistence and perseverance | 充满韧性、不屈不挠 |

## Exercises

*Directions: Decide whether the following statements are true (T) or false (F) according to the information in the passage.*

1. Those who learn martial arts need to cultivate such fine qualities as justice, diligence and persistence and so on.  (    )
2. Chinese Wushu can display the oriental civilization.  (    )

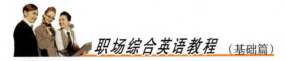

3. A person who doesn't value martial ethics is not a real man practicing martial arts. (　)
4. In ancient China, it was for protecting the homeland that Wushu took birth. (　)
5. The practice of martial arts has little impact on a person's life. (　)
6. Martial skills are more important than moral ethics in learning Wushu. (　)

*Directions: Guess the meanings of the words and phrases in the box according to the passage. Then, use them to complete the following sentences, changing the form if necessary.*

| respect for | learn from | aim at | care for |
|---|---|---|---|
| evaluate | maintain | emphasis on | cooperate with |

1. We should put _____ learning the spoken language.
2. I have the greatest _____ your parents.
3. She moved back home to _____ her elderly parents.
4. The two teams agreed to _____ each other.
5. The government is _____ a 50% reduction in unemployment.
6. The two countries have always _____ close relations.
7. We need to _____ how well the policy is working.
8. I _____ a lot _____ my father.

*Directions: Pay attention to different parts of speech and select the appropriate word to fill in the blanks.*

1. cooperate   cooperation   cooperative
   a. As a member of the team, first we should learn to _____ with others.
   b. We should be grateful for your _____ in clearing the hall as quickly as possible.
   c. _____ activity is essential to effective office work.
2. person   personal   personally   personality
   a. He is just the _____ we need for the job.
   b. Of course, this is just a _____ opinion.
   c. _____, I prefer the second one.
   d. Her husband has a strong _____.
3. value   valuable   valuables   valuation
   a. This advice was to prove _____.
   b. Please put the _____ in a safe.
   c. Houses tend to hold their _____ well.
   d. Experts set a high _____ on the painting.
4. honest   honesty   honestly
   a. Thank you for being so _____ with me.
   b. I can't believe he got that money _____.
   c. She answered all my questions with her usual _____.

• Unit 3  Sports •

*Directions: First translate the following English sentences into Chinese. Then, pay attention to the italicized parts in the English sentences and translate the Chinese sentences by simulating the structure of the English sentences.*

1. *Generally speaking*, it evaluates man's behaviour with such conceptions as the good and evil, justice and injustice, and honesty and dishonesty.
   一般说来，老板是通过这样一些品质来评价员工的，如守时、勤奋、团队精神。

2. In ancient China, human beings *were regarded as* the most valuable treasure of nature.
   人们普遍认为他是最成功的歌手。

3. *It was for* protecting and maintaining human life *that* Wushu took birth.
   正是为了健身和减肥才有了瑜伽。

4. *While learning* martial skills, one should also cultivate the fine qualities.
   在等公交时，我习惯听音乐。

5. *Those who* learn martial arts should *keep improving* their skills and learn from each other to improve and be united and cooperative with each other.
   学外语的人要坚持操练听说技能。

6. More principles *provide* the basis *for* maintaining a stable relationship between man and man, and between man and society.
   我们来这里是为公众服务。

*Directions: Group activity.*
Discussing the following questions:
1. How do you understand Olympic spirit?
   Cooperation ＊ Honour ＊ Fairness
   High moral and physical standards
2. Do you like to play sports? Name just one sport which can be described by the following words.

| dull | impressive | boring | fast-moving | dangerous |
| slow | thrilling | exciting | violent | spectacular |

## Part IV  Grammar

## 名词和代词

### 一、名词的用法

名词可以分为专有名词和普通名词,专有名词是某个(些)人,地方,机构等专有的名称,如 Beijing, China 等。普通名词是一类人或东西或是一个抽象概念的名词,如:book, sadness 等。普通名词又可分为下面四类:

1) 个体名词:表示某类人或东西中的个体,如:gun。
2) 集体名词:表示若干个个体组成的集合体,如:family。
3) 物质名词:表示无法分为个体的实物,如:air。
4) 抽象名词:表示动作、状态、品质、感情等抽象概念,如:work。

个体名词和集体名词可以用数目来计算,称为可数名词,物质名词和抽象名词一般无法用数目计算,称为不可数名词。

**1. 名词复数的规则变化**

| 情况 | 构成方法 | 读音 | 例词 |
| --- | --- | --- | --- |
| 一般情况 | 加 -s | 清辅音后读 /s/<br>浊辅音和元音后读 /z/ | map-maps<br>bag-bags /car-cars |
| 以 s, sh, ch, x 等结尾 | 加 -es | /iz/ | bus-buses/ watch-watches |
| 以 ce, se, ze, 等结尾 | 加 -s | /iz/ | license-licenses |
| 以辅音字母+y 结尾 | 变 y 为 i 再加 es | /z/ | baby-babies |

**2. 其它名词复数的规则变化**

1) 以 y 结尾的专有名词,或元音字母+y 结尾的名词变复数时,直接加 s 变复数。如:

> two Marys            the Henrys
> monkey—monkeys       holiday—holidays

2) 以 o 结尾的名词,变复数时:

> a. 加 s,如: photo—photos     piano—pianos
>               radio—radios       zoo—zoos
> b. 加 es,如: potato—potatoes   tomato—tomatoes
> c. 上述 a 和 b 两种方法均可,如 zero—zeros / zeroes。

3) 以 f 或 fe 结尾的名词变复数时：

  a. 加 s，如：belief—beliefs  roof—roofs
        safe—safes   gulf—gulfs；
  b. 去 f 或 fe 加 ves，如：half—halves
        knife—knives leaf—leaves wolf—wolves
        wife—wives  life—lives  thief—thieves；

3. 名词复数的不规则变化

1) child—children foot—feet  tooth—teeth
  mouse—mice  man—men  woman—women

**注意**：由一个词加 man 或 woman 构成的合成词，其复数形式也是 -men 和 -women，如：an Englishman，two Englishmen。但 German 不是合成词，故复数形式为 Germans；Bowman 是姓，其复数是 the Bowmans。

2) 单复同形，如 deer, sheep, fish, Chinese, Japanese , li, jin, yuan, two li, three mu, four jin 等。但除人民币的元、角、分外，美元、英镑、法郎等都有复数形式。如：a dollar, two dollars；a meter, two meters。

3) 集体名词，以单数形式出现，但实为复数。例如：
people, police, cattle 等本身就是复数，不能说 a people，a police，a cattle，但可以说 a person, a policeman, a head of cattle, the English, the British, the French, the Chinese, the Japanese, the Swiss 等名词，表示国民总称时，作复数用，如 The Chinese are industrious and brave. 中国人民是勤劳勇敢的。

4) 以 s 结尾，仍为单数的名词，如：
  a. maths, politics, physics 等学科名词，一般是不可数名词，为单数。
  b. news 为不可数名词。
  c. the United States, the United Nations 应视为单数。
   The United Nations was organized in 1945. 联合国是 1945 年组建起来的。
  d. 以复数形式出现的书名，剧名，报纸，杂志名，也可视为单数。如：
   *The Arabian Nights* is a very interesting story-book.
   《一千零一夜》是一本非常有趣的故事书。

5) 表示由两部分构成的东西，如：glasses（眼镜），trousers，clothes 等，若表达具体数目，要借助数量词 pair（对，双）；suit（套）；a pair of glasses；two pairs of trousers 等。

6) 另外还有一些名词，其复数形式有时可表示特别意思，如：goods 货物，waters 水域，fishes（各种）鱼。

4. 名词的格

英语中有些名词可以用"'s"来表示所有关系，带这种词尾的名词形式称为该名词的所有格，如：a teacher's book。名词所有格的规则如下：

1) 单数名词词尾加"'s"，复数名词词尾没有 s，也要加"'s"，如：the boy's bag 男孩的书

包,men's room 男厕所。

2) 若名词已有复数词尾-s,只加"'",如:the workers' struggle 工人的斗争。

3) 凡不能加"'s"的名词,都可以用"名词+of+名词"的结构来表示所有关系,如:the title of the song 歌的名字。

4) 在表示店铺或教堂的名字或某人的家时,名词所有格的后面常常不出现它所修饰的名词,如:the barber's 理发店。

5) 如果两个名词并列,并且分别有"'s",则表示"分别有";只有一个"'s",则表示"共有"。如:

John's and Mary's rooms(两间)　　John and Mary's room(一间)

6)复合名词或短语,"'s"加在最后一个词的词尾。如:a month or two's absence

## 二、代词的用法

代词是代替名词、形容词和数词的词。按其意义、特征及其在句中的作用分为:人称代词、物主代词、指示代词、反身代词、相互代词、疑问代词、不定代词和关系代词等。

### 1. 人称代词

表示"我"、"你"、"他"、"她"、"它"、"我们"、"你们"、"他们"的词。人称代词有人称、数和格的变化如下:

| 数 | 单数 | | 复数 | |
| --- | --- | --- | --- | --- |
| 格 | 主格 | 宾格 | 主格 | 宾格 |
| 第一人称 | I | me | we | us |
| 第二人称 | you | you | you | you |
| 第三人称 | he | him | they | them |
| | she | her | they | them |
| | it | it | they | them |

### 2. 物主代词

表示所有关系的代词叫物主代词。物主代词分形容词性物主代词和名词性物主代词。
其人物和数的变化如下:

| 数 | 单数 | | | 复数 | | |
| --- | --- | --- | --- | --- | --- | --- |
| 人称 | 第一人称 | 第二人称 | 第三人称 | 第一人称 | 第二人称 | 第三人称 |
| 形容词性物主代词 | my | your | his/her | our | your | their |
| 名词性物主代词 | mine | yours | his/hers | ours | yours | theirs |

Our school is here, and theirs is there.(作主语)

I've already finished my homework. Have you finished yours?(作宾语)

3. 指示代词

指示代词包括:this,that,these,those。

This is a pen and that is a pencil.

What I want to say is this: pronunciation is very important in learning English.

Hello! This is Mary. Is that Jack speaking?

4. 反身代词

英语中用来表示"我自己","你自己","他自己","我们自己","你们自己"等意义的代词称为反身代词,也有人称之为自身代名词,如:myself, yourself, himself, ourselves, yourselves等。

He called himself a writer.

The girl in the news is myself.

5. 不定代词

不是指明代替任何特定名词的代词叫做不定代词,在句中可作主语、表语、宾语和定语。如:some,any,few,a few,little,a little,other,the other,another,others,the others,each,every,all,both等。

Look! Some of the students are cleaning the library.

They had little money with them.

In our class only Tom is English, the others are Chinese.

The teacher gave a toy to each child.

Lucy and Lily both agree with us.

6. 相互代词

表示相互关系的代词叫做相互代词。相互代词有 each other 和 one another 两种形式。在当代英语中,each other 和 one another 没有什么区别。相互代词可在句中作宾语,定语。作定语用时,相互代词用所有格形式。

We should learn from each other / one another.(作宾语)

Do you often write to each other / one another? (作宾语)

We often borrow each other's / one another's books. (作定语)

7. 疑问代词

疑问代词有 who,whom,whose,what 和 which 等。疑问代词用于特殊疑问句中,一般都放在句首,并在句子中作为某一句子成分。如:

Who is going to come here tomorrow?(作主语)

Whose umbrella is this? (作定语)

Whom are you waiting for? (作宾语)

8. 关系代词

关系代词是一种引导从句并起连接主句和从句作用的代词。关系代词有 who, whose, whom, that, which. 它们在句中可用作主语,表语,宾语,定语;它们还代表着从句所修饰的那个名词或代词。如:

I hate people who talk much but do little.

I'm looking at the photograph which you sent me with your letter.

Do you know the lady who is interviewing our headmaster?

## Exercises

*Directions: There are 10 incomplete statements here. You are required to complete each statement by choosing the appropriate answer from the 4 choices marked A, B, C and D.*

1. —Are those _____?
   —No, they aren't. They're _____.
   A. sheep; cows        B. sheep; cow
   C. sheeps; cow        D. sheeps; cows

2. Mum, I'm quite thirsty. Please give me _____.
   A. two orange         B. two bottles of orange
   C. two bottles orange D. two bottles of oranges

3. I have got _____ news from my friend. Do you want to know?
   A. a very good        B. any
   C. a piece of         D. two pieces

4. _____ room is on the 5th floor.
   A. Lucy and Lily      B. Lucy and Lily's
   C. Lucy's and Lily    D. Lucy's and Lily's

5. Every morning Mr. Smith takes a _____ to his office.
   A. 20 minutes' walk   B. 20 minute's walk
   C. 20-minutes walk    D. 20-minute walk

6. This is James Allan Green. We can call him _____.
   A. Mr. Green          B. Mr. Allan
   C. Mr. James          D. James Green

7. Jack and Tom are _____.
   A. good friends       B. good friend
   C. a good friend      D. good a friend

8. It's only about ten _____ walk to the nearest post office.
   A. minutes            B. minute's
   C. minutes'           D. minute

9. He often has _____ for breakfast.
   A. two breads         B. two piece of breads
   C. two pieces of bread D. two pieces of breads

10. Mrs. Green has two _____. They're very bright.
   A. childs           B. child
   C. children's       D. children

Directions: There are 5 incomplete statements here. You are required to complete each statement by choosing the appropriate answer from the 4 choices marked A, B, C, D.

1. David's words are different from _____. I really can't agree with _____.
   A. mine; him    B. mine; he's    C. me; him    D. me; his
2. —Can you speak Chinese?
   —Yes. But only _____.
   A. Few          B. a few         C. Little     D. a little
3. —Can I talk to you for a minute, Aggie?
   —Sorry, I have _____ time.
   A. a few        B. little        C. few        D. a little
4. Does _____ matter if you can't find your English book?
   A. it           B. this          C. that       D. he
5. Your friend is from England, but _____ is from America.
   A. my           B. her           C. his        D. our

## Part V  Applied Writing

### Lost and Found (寻物启事与失物招领)

寻物启事是个人或单位丢失物品，希望通过启事得到帮助找回物品的一种应用文。失物招领则是个人或单位拾到丢失的物品，希望通过启事得到帮助找到物品的所有者的一种应用文。一般可张贴于丢失物品或拾到物品的地点，或贴在单位门口或街巷较显眼的位置，有的也刊登在报纸杂志上。

Sample 1:

### A Briefcase Found

Dec.12, 2011

A briefcase was found, inside of which are money and other things. Owner is expected to come to identify it. Please apply at the lost property office. Open from 8:00 to 11:00 a.m. and 2:30 p.m. to 5:30 p.m..

## 公文包招领

　　拾到公文包一个,内有现金及其他物品。遗失者请于每日上午 8:00—11:00 或下午 2:30—5:30,到失物招领处认领。

2011.12.12

Sample 2:

| Found: watch. | Lost |
| --- | --- |
| Is this your watch? | My school ID card. |
| Please call Li Chao. | My name is Tony. |
| Phone number at 688997. | Please call 685-6034. |

### Basic Expressions(常用表达)

Lost:　　　　　　　　　　　Found:
My ... is lost.　　　　　　　Is this your ...
My name is ...　　　　　　　My name is ...
Please call at ...　　　　　　Please call at ...

## Exercises

*Directions: Fill in the blanks in the following English notice so that it is functionally equivalent to the Chinese version.*

## 寻物启事

　　昨天我在图书馆丢了一个黄色的手袋,里面有我的宿舍和自行车钥匙、学生证、笔、还有一些钱,这些东西对于我很重要。无论谁捡到了,希望能够尽快还给我。我将十分感激!

　　我叫萧红,三年级二班的学生。可以直接到班里找我,也可以打电话,号码是8883434。非常感谢!

## Lost

I _____ a yellow handbag in the school library yesterday. There are the keys \_\_\_\_ my bedroom and my bike, my student ID card, pens and some money in the small bag. These things are very important to me. _____ finds it, I wish he/she would be kind \_\_\_\_\_ to return it to me as soon as _____. I will be very \_\_\_\_\_!

My name is Xiao Hong, Class Two of Grade Three. Come to my classroom \_\_\_ or give me a _____. My telephone number is 8883434. Thank you very much!

*Directions: This part is to test your ability to do practical writing. You are required to write a Found and a Lost based on the following information given in Chinese.*

说明：

失物招领：王平拾到一个笔记本，电话234-3587。

寻物启事：李飞丢了身份证，电话3201589。

寻物启事：Lost:

失物招领：Found:

## Part VI  Cultural Express

### Ding Junhui, the Easy-going Snooker Superstar

*Egan Richardson*

It's easy to forget that Ding is just 23, given that he has been a celebrity for nearly a decade now.

The expectations following his China Open (斯诺克中国公开赛) win were huge, and the peaks and troughs in a young player's form have frustrated his more excitable followers, but are an integral part of any young players' development.

In 2007 the teenaged Ding got to the final of the UK Masters (英国温布利斯诺克大师赛), where he met one of the most talented players in the history of the game, Ronnie O'Sullivan (奥沙利文). A raucous crowd cheered on Sullivan to a 10-3 win, and left the young Ding in tears. Three years later, the sensitive and talented Ding has worked out how to play without worrying about the crowd's reactions.

"That's something I've learned," says Ding. "I know, as Stephen Hendry(亨德利) told me before, that every player has to learn about this. When I was young, maybe I didn't know this, but after this, I know

how to deal with it, and how to play snooker with a crowd. Sometimes you need people in the crowd not to always keep quiet, then it's not interesting and people don't want to watch the sport. A lot of people like football because they are always shouting, because the crowd are working every day and sport is just for fun. I will give them the best opportunity to show that they are enjoying their snooker, so that's good."

His easy-going nature shines through in his relaxed response to a query about targets for the new season.

"I'm not sure how good I can play this season," says the Yixing (中国宜兴) native. "I'll just try my best every game. Just do my best, that's okay. When I play a snooker match, I feel happy, I feel good, and that's it for me."

Ding's victories, of course, have the potential to make many more people happy. The Asian market is now regarded as crucial for snooker's future.

"Most people love snooker in Asia," says Ding. "It's a big market for snooker. Snooker is going to be a worldwide sport. Chinese people love to watch the World Championship, because it's the most important tournament of the year, so everyone is looking for that tournament."

The possibility of Sheffield's (英国谢菲尔德市) most cherished snooker event moving on is not something the city would welcome, but if anyone can help pull it off, its the mild mannered man from Yixing.

# 拓展词汇

### 田径

track 径赛；110m hurdles 110米栏；3,000m steeple chase 3000米障碍赛；4x100m relay 4×100米接力；high jump 跳高；pole vault 撑杆跳高；long jump 跳远；triple jump 三级跳远；throwing 投掷；shot put 推铅球；discus 掷铁饼；hammer 掷链球；javelin 标枪；decathlon 男子十项全能；heptathlon 女子七项全能；marathon 马拉松

### 球类

badminton 羽毛球；men's singles 男子单打；women's singles 女子单打；men's doubles 男子双打；women's doubles 女子双打；mixed doubles 混合双打；handball 手球；hockey/field hockey 曲棍球；beach volleyball 沙滩排球

### 游泳

swimming 游泳；freestyle 自由泳；backstroke 仰泳；breaststroke 蛙泳；butterfly 蝶泳；individual medley 个人混合泳；freestyle relay 自由泳接力；medley relay 混合泳接力

### 跳水

10m platform event 十米跳台；3m springboard event 三米跳板；synchronized diving from 10m platform 双人十米跳台；synchronized diving from 3m springboard 双人三米跳板；synchronized swimming 花样游泳

### 体操

artistic gymnastics 竞技体操；floor exercises 自由体操；pommel horse 鞍马；rings 吊环；vault 跳马；parallel bars 双杠；horizontal bar 单杠；uneven bars 高低杠；balance beam 平衡木；rhythmic gymnastics 艺术体操；gymnastics trampoline 蹦床

### 自行车

road cycling 公路自行车赛；track cycling 场地自行车赛；sprint 追逐赛；time trial 计时赛；points race 计分赛；pursuit 争先赛 mountain bike 山地自行车赛

### 举重

snatch 抓举；clean and jerk 挺举

### 摔跤

greco-roman 古典式摔跤；freestyle 自由式摔跤

### 马术

jumping 障碍赛；dressage 盛装舞步；eventing 三日赛

## Unit 3  Sports

**射箭**
individual events 个人赛; team events 团体赛

**击剑**
foil 花剑; epee 重剑; sabre 佩剑

**现代五项**
shooting 射击; fencing 击剑; swimming 游泳; riding 马术; cross-country running 越野跑

# Unit 4

# Food Culture

**Learning Objectives:**

You are able to:

☞ Identify some basic sounds of letters

☞ Use proper expressions to comment on food culture

☞ Know the use of adjectives & adverbs

☞ Write notes

You are suggested to:

☞ Be familiar with some food culture

## Unit 4  Food Culture

If you want to understand the food of Western countries, it is necessary to discuss some aspects of Western culture, history, geography and local customs. Two major factors will influence the formation and development of the food culture of a nation: one is regionalism; the other is the diversity of human factors.

## Part I  Phonetics

### Task 1  Identifying Their Pronunciations

*Directions: Listen to the following words and read after the speaker, paying attention to the colored parts.*

| /ɪə/ | /ɛː/ | /uə/ | /əʊ/ | /aʊ/ |
|---|---|---|---|---|
| /r/ | /tr/ | /dr/ | /tʃ/ | /dʒ/ |

| | | | | |
|---|---|---|---|---|
| (1) here | dear | beer | cereal | fierce |
| (2) pear | their | there | fair | care |
| (3) usually | sure | surely | surety | mature |
| (4) go | blow | over | those | coat |
| (5) out | about | how | now | our |
| (6) row | ride | borrow | wrong | report |
| (7) tree | true | truce | truck | trust |
| (8) dress | draw | hundred | drive | dream |
| (9) choose | chip | catch | each | French |
| (10) jade | joke | judge | bridge | vegetable |

**Practice:** Write down the sound of the underlined part of the words

<u>ch</u>air     <u>dr</u>iver     <u>tr</u>ousers     b<u>oa</u>t     <u>o</u>range

_____     _____     _____     _____     _____

### Task 2　Appreciating a Poem

*Directions: Listen to an English version of the poem "A Welcome Rain One Spring Night". Choose the words you hear to fill in the blanks.*

| | | | |
|---|---|---|---|
| **slip** | /slɪp/ | v. | 滑，滑倒 |
| **moisten** | /ˈmɔɪs(ə)n/ | v. | （使变得）潮湿，变得湿润 |
| **shed** | /ʃɛd/ | n. | 棚，库 |
| | | v. | 流出，流下 |
| **glimmer** | /ˈglɪmə/ | n. | 微光，闪光 |
| | | v. | 闪烁，发微光 |
| **splash** | /splaʃ/ | n. | 溅泼声，溅上的斑点，溅泼的量 |
| **drench** | /drɛn(t)ʃ/ | v. | 使湿透 |
| **brocade** | /brəˈkeɪd/ | n. | 凸花纹织物，锦缎 |

> Poem　　　　A Welcome Rain One Spring Night
>
> *Du Fu*
>
> A good rain _____ (knows, nose) its season.
> And comes when spring is here;
> On the _____ (hills, heels) of the wind it _____ (sleeps, slips) secretly into the night,
> Silent and soft, it moistens _____ (every thing, everything).
> Now clouds _____ (hang, ham) black above the country roads,
> A _____ (lone, low) boat on the river sheds a glimmer of light;
> At _____ (dawn, door) we shall see splashes of rain-washed red
> Drenched, heavy _____ (blue, blooms) in the City of Brocade.

### Task 3  Time for Fun: Tongue Twister

*Directions: Practise the tongue twister sentence by sentence after the speaker. Pay attention to the sounds.*

(1) Fred baked red bread during the break.

(2) She sells seashells on the seashore. The shells she sells are seashells, she is sure.

(3) How many cookies could a good cook cook if a good cook could cook cookies? A good cook could cook as many cookies as a good cook who could cook cookies.

## Part II  Listening and Speaking

### Task 1  Short Dialogues

*Directions: Listen to the following short dialogues and fill in the blanks with the information you get from the recording. Each dialogue will be read twice.*

(1) **W:** Mr. Smith, what kind of _____ do you like best?
   **M:** Well, I like _____.

(2) **W:** And do you know _____?
   **M:** Yes, the brief _____ of it has always been the _____ to find the _____ best coffees.

(3) **W:** When did it open?
   **M:** In _____.

(4) **W:** The name comes from Herman Melville's Moby Dick, a _____ American novel.
   **M:** Yes, I know it. It is a novel about the 19th century _____ industry.

(5) **W:** In how many countries does the company have _____ today?
   **M:** As far as I know, today the company has more than _____ _____ in more than _____ countries.

### Task 2  Answering the Questions

*Directions: You will hear 5 recorded questions. Listen carefully and choose the proper answer to each question. The questions will be read twice.*

(1) A. A famous opera.             B. An American brand of ice cream.
   C. Yes, I like it.              D. A book.

(2) A. Hot dogs and rice dumplings.  B. Pop corn and hamburgers.
   C. Hot dogs, hamburgers and Coca-cola.  D. Hot dogs and hamburgers.

(3) A. In China and Korea.          B. In Japan and America.
   C. In America and Canada.        D. In Canada and Italy.

(4) A. In Atlanta.    B. In England.
    C. In Paris.      D. In Tokyo.
(5) A. Good taste.    B. The history of Coke.
    C. The price of Coke.    D. Promotion from the early years to present days.

### Task 3  Oral Practice

*Warm-Up 1: Match the expressions in the left column with the expressions in the right column so as to form 7 short dialogues.*

| | |
|---|---|
| (1) —Do you know Coca-cola? | —I like coffee best. |
| (2) —What's your favourite drink? | —Ice cream, of course. |
| (3) —Is there anything I can do for you? | —A popular soft drink invented in America. |
| (4) —What do you know about Häagen-Dazs? | —Yes, I ate rice dumpling wrapped in reed leaves. |
| (5) —What food do you think is popular among kids in summer? | —A bottle of beer. |
| (6) —What food do Chinese people like eating on the Mid-Autumn Festival? | —They like moon cakes. |
| (7) —Did you eat rice dumplings? | —A famous brand of ice cream. |

*Warm-Up 2: Work with your partner to praltise the following useful expressions.*

**If you are a waiter/waitress in a restaurant, you can say**
(1) Can I help you?
(2) What can I do for you?
(3) What would you like to eat?
(4) What do you want to drink?

**If you are a customer, you can say**
(1) Could you please show me some...?
(2) Could you please give me a menu?
(3) I'd like to drink ....
(4) A cup of coffee.

## Unit 4  Food Culture

**Dialogue**

*Li Hong from China and Mrs. Brown from America are friends. They are talking about corporate culture.*

Li Hong:     Nice to meet you, Mrs. Brown.
Mrs. Brown: Nice to meet you, too.
Li Hong:     Where do you live now?
Mrs. Brown: In Atlanta, Georgia.
Li Hong:     As far as I know, Coca-cola was born there.
Mrs. Brown: Yes, Coca-Cola was born in Atlanta, Georgia in 1886.
Li Hong:     It has a long history. Coca-cola is a famous brand. So many people in the world like it. Could you please introduce the history of Coca-cola briefly for me?
Mrs. Brown: Yes, I'd like to. A local pharmacist, Dr John Styth Pemberton invented the drink at his home. His partner first used the now famous trademark "Coca-Cola". The first year, sales averaged 9 drinks per day. Each drink sold for 5 cents. Today billions of gallons are consumed each year. "Coke" for short, is sold in 155 countries around the world. To protect the trade name, "Coca-Cola, Coke," and even the "familiar shaped bottle" are registered trademarks.
Li Hong:     So exciting.
Mrs. Brown: Creative slogans throughout the years have kept Coca-Cola "king of hill". Do you know some of the slogans which have made Coca-Cola forever famous?
Li Hong:     Yes, I know some from advertisements, such as *Delicious and Refreshing*, *Global High Sign*, *Catch the Wave*, *Always Coca-Cola* and so on.

### New Words and Expressions

| | | | |
|---|---|---|---|
| Coca-Cola | /ˌkəʊkəˈkəʊlə/ | n. | 可口可乐 |
| pharmacist | /ˈfɑːməsɪst/ | n. | 药剂师 |
| partner | /ˈpɑːtnə/ | n. | 伙伴,同伙,搭档 |
| trademark | /ˈtreɪdmɑːk/ | n. | (注册)商标 |
| creative | /kriːˈeɪtɪv/ | adj. | 创造性的,有创造力的 |
| slogan | /ˈsləʊɡ(ə)n/ | n. | 标语,口号,广告语 |
| delicious and refreshing | | | 美味怡神 |
| Global High Sign | | | 全球欢腾 |
| Catch the Wave | | | 赶浪潮 |
| Always Coca-Cola | | | 永远的可口可乐 |

## Task 4  Role Play

(1) Imagine you are a tourist guide and now you are introducing Starbucks History to the visitors. Make up a dialogue between a visitor and you. The patterns you learned just now and the expressions given below may be of some help to you.

| Expressions | |
|---|---|
| Welcome to ... | 欢迎来到…… |
| Brief introduction to ... | 简单介绍…… |
| What do you know about ...? | 你对……了解多少? |

(2) Now you come to a bar. You want to buy something to drink. The assistant serves you. Make up a dialogue according to the information. The patterns you learned just now and the expressions given below may be of some help to you.

| Expressions | | | |
|---|---|---|---|
| alcohol | /ˈalkəhɔl/ | n. | 酒,酒精,含酒精的饮料 |
| What can I do for you? | | | 需要我为你做点什么吗? |
| Would you like some to drink? | | | 您要喝点什么吗? |

## Task 5  Leisure Time: Learning to Sing a Song

1. Listen to the song "You raise me up".
2. Listen to the song again and fill in the missing words.

### You raise me up

When I am down and, oh my soul, so weary;
When troubles come and my heart burdened be;
Then, I am still and wait here in the_____,
Until you come and sit awhile with me.
You raise me up, so I can stand on_____;
You raise me up, to walk on _____ seas;
I am strong, when I am on your _____;
You raise me up... to more than I can be .
You raise me up, so I can stand on mountains;

You raise me up, to walk on stormy seas;
I am strong, when I am on your shoulders;
You raise me up... to more than I can be.

There is no life—no life without its _____;
Each restless heart beats so imperfectly;
But when you come and I am filled with _____,
Sometimes, I think I glimpse eternity.
You raise me up, so I can

• Unit 4  Food Culture •

stand on mountains;
You raise me up, to walk on stormy seas;
And I am strong, when I am on your shoulders;
You raise me up... to more than I can be.
You raise me up... to more than I can be.

You raise me up, so I can stand on mountains;
You raise me up, to walk on stormy seas;
I am_____, when I am on your shoulders;
You raise me up: To more than I can be.

3. Learn to sing the song after the singer.

# Part III  Reading

**Text A**

## Our Heritage

Every day, we go to work hoping to do two things: share great coffee with our friends and help make the world a little better. It was true when the first Starbucks opened in 1971, and it's just as true today.

Back then, the company was a single store in Seattle's historic Pike Place Market. From just a narrow storefront, Starbucks offered some of the world's finest fresh-roasted whole bean coffees. The name, inspired by *Moby Dick*, evoked the romance of the high seas and the seafaring tradition of the early coffee traders.

In 1981, Howard Schultz, later chairman of the company, walked into a Starbucks store for the first time and he joined a year later because of his first cup of Sumatra there.

A year later, in 1983, Howard traveled to Italy and became captivated with Italian coffee bars and the romance of the coffee experience. He had a vision to bring the Italian coffeehouse tradition back to the United States. It should be a place for conversation and a sense of community, a third place between work and home. He left Starbucks for a short period of time to start his own coffeehouses and returned in August 1987 to purchase Starbucks with the help of local investors.

From the beginning, Starbucks set out to be a different kind of company, one that not only celebrated coffee and the rich tradition, but also brought a feeling of connection.

Today, with more than 15,000 stores in 50 countries, Starbucks is the premier roaster

and retailer of specialty coffee in the world. And with every cup, they strive to bring both their heritage and an exceptional experience to life.

### New Words

| | | | |
|---|---|---|---|
| ☆heritage | /ˈhɛrɪtɪdʒ/ | n. | 遗产，继承物 |
| ★roast | /rəʊst/ | v. | 烤，烘，焙 |
| ☆evoke | /ɪˈvəʊk/ | n. | 产生，引起，唤起 |
| seafaring | /ˈsiːfɛːrɪŋ/ | n. | 航海的，水上的 |
| ★captivate | /ˈkæptɪveɪt/ | v. | 迷住，迷惑 |
| ★vision | /ˈvɪʒ(ə)n/ | n. | 视力，想像力 |
| ★investor | /ɪnˈvɛst/ | n. | 投资者，出资者 |
| retailer | /ˈriːteɪlə/ | n. | 零售商，零售店 |
| ★specialty | /ˈspɛʃ(ə)lti/ | n. | 特制品 |
| ☆strive | /strʌɪv/ | v. | 努力奋斗，力求 |
| ☆exceptional | /ɪkˈsɛpʃ(ə)n(ə)l, ɛk-/ | adj. | 杰出的，例外的，独特的 |

### Phrases and Expressions

| | |
|---|---|
| because of | 由于 |
| become captivated with | 对……痴迷 |
| bring back | 带回 |
| set out to | 开始做 |
| not only... but also | 不但……而且…… |
| strive to do | 努力…… |

### Proper Names

| | | | |
|---|---|---|---|
| Starbucks | | | 星巴克 |
| Seattle | /sɪˈat(ə)l/ | n. | 西雅图 |
| Pike Place Market | | | 派克市场 |
| Moby Dick | | | 白鲸 |
| Sumatra | /sʊˈmɑːtrə/ | n. | （此处指）苏门答腊咖啡 |

# Unit 4  Food Culture

## Exercises

*Directions: Answer the following questions according to the passage.*

1. According to the writer, what two things do we have to do when going to work?
2. When and where did the first Starbucks open?
3. What was Starbucks named for?
4. Did Howard Schultz join Starbucks because of his nice impression on his first cup of Sumatra?
5. What decision did he make after he travelled to Italy?
6. What unusual experience can customers have in Starbucks?

*Directions: Choose the best meaning of each italicized word according to the context and try to tell how you get the answer.*

1. The name, inspired by Moby Dick (《白鲸》), *evoked* the romance of the high seas and the seafaring tradition of the early coffee traders.
   A. 唤醒　　B. 使……想起　C. 引起
2. A year later, Howard traveled to Italy and became *captivated* with Italian coffee bars and the romance of the coffee experience.
   A. 被迷住　B. 被捕获　　C. 被抓住
3. He had a *vision* to bring the Italian coffeehouse tradition back to the United States
   A. 视力　　B. 视野　　　C. 想法
4. From the beginning, Starbucks *set out* to be a different kind of company.
   A. 出发　　B. 开始努力做　C. 陈列
5. Starbucks is the *premier* roaster and retailer of specialty coffee in the world.
   A. 首要的　B. 总理的　　C. 最初的

## Vocabulary

*Directions: Match each word in column A with its definition in Column B*

| Column A | Column B |
|---|---|
| 1. fresh-roasted | a. be attracted deeply |
| 2. evoke | b. a type of food that a restaurant or an area is well-known for |
| 3. be captivated with | c. someone who gives money to a business to get a profit |
| 4. vision | d. unusually good, outstanding |
| 5. investor | e. to produce a strong feeling or memory of |
| 6. retailer | f. to make a great effort to achieve one's goals |
| 7. strive | g. an idea of what you think something should be like |
| 8. exceptional | h. a person or business that sells something |
| 9. specialty | i. having just been made |
| 10. heritage | j. the traditional beliefs, values, customs |

*Directions: Complete the following sentences with words from Column A above. Change the form where necessary.*

1. The president had a clear _____ of how he hoped the company would develop.
2. I was still _____ to be successful.
3. Amazon.com is the world's most popular _____ on the Internet.
4. The photographs _____ strong memories of our holidays in France.
5. The Chinese present policies attract a lot of foreign _____.
6. Mrs. Smith always buys _____ bread in a neighboring store.
7. Waiter, would you please recommend some _____ in this restaurant?
8. It's very important to preserve its cultural _____.
9. John Smith is named the _____ manager this year.
10. Many visitors are _____ the wonderful scenery of the West Lake.

*Directions: Translate the following sentences into English.*

1. The area's beautiful scenery _____ (激发了) numerous artists' imagination.
2. It is impossible to _____ (使人人都喜欢你).
3. The Chinese Tele-communication System _____ (开始为提供更好的服务而努力).
4. China is _____ (有着丰富的文化遗产).
5. She is such an exceptional that she _____ (被提升了两次) in six months.
6. Reading can _____ (提高你的语言能力).

Text B

## Made Like No Other

Reuben Mattus, a young businessman with an idea of creating the finest ice cream, worked in his mother's ice cream business selling fruit ice and ice cream pops from a wagon in the noisy streets of the Bronx, New York. To produce the finest ice cream, he insisted on using only the finest, purest ingredients.

The family business prospered throughout the 1930's, 40's and 50's. By 1960, Mr. Mattus, decided to form a new company and he called his new brand Häagen-Dazs. Häagen-Dazs started out with only three flavors: vanilla, chocolate and coffee.

In 1983 Mr. Mattus agreed to sell Häagen-Dazs to The Pillsbury Company, which kept the tradition of superior quality on which Häagen-Dazs was founded. Since then, it has become a global phenomenon and it can be bought in 50 countries. Ice Cream lovers all over the world now regard Häagen-Dazs as the representative of super-quality ice cream.

Since the beginning, Häagen-Dazs has tried to bring new frozen dessert experiences to its customers, including special flavors such as Vanilla Swiss Almond, Butter Pecan and Dulce de Leche, to name just a few. Other super high-class innovations followed, with Frozen Yogurt in 1991 and Sorbet in 1993.

To this day, Häagen-Dazs remains committed to developing exceptional new high-level frozen dessert experiences, releasing new flavors every year.

### New Words

| pure | /pjʊə/ | adj. | 纯的,纯净的 |
| ☆ingredient | /ɪnˈɡriːdiənt/ | n. | (混合物的)组成部分,(烹调的)原料 |
| ★prosper | /ˈprɒspə/ | v. | 繁盛,成功 |
| flavor | /ˈfleɪvə/ | n. | 味,香料 |
| vanilla | /vəˈnɪlə/ | n. | 香草 |

| | | | |
|---|---|---|---|
| superior | /suːˈpɪərɪə, sjuː-/ | adj. | （在质量等方面）较好的 |
| ★representative | /reprɪˈzentətɪv/ | n. | 代表，类似物 |
| ☆almond | /ˈɑːmənd/ | n. | 杏树，杏仁 |
| ☆pecan | /ˈpiːk(ə)n, pɪˈkan, pɪˈkɑːn/ | n. | 美洲山核桃 |
| ☆innovation | /ɪnəˈveɪʃ(ə)n/ | n. | 创新，新发明 |
| yogurt | /ˈjɒgət, ˈjəʊ-/ | n. | 酸奶，酸乳酪 |
| ★commit | /kəˈmɪt/ | v. | 保证（做某事、遵守协议或遵从安排等），承诺 |
| ★release | /rɪˈliːs/ | v. | 释放，发行 |

## Phrases and Expressions

| | |
|---|---|
| fruit ice | 水果冰沿 |
| ice cream pops | 雪糕 |
| insist on | 坚持 |
| start out | 开始 |
| all over the world | 全世界 |
| to name just a few | 仅举几例 |
| get/be committed to | 承诺，保证（做某事、遵守协议或遵从安排等） |

## Proper Names

| | | | |
|---|---|---|---|
| Bronx | /brɒŋks/ | n. | 布朗克斯（纽约市最北端的一区） |
| Häagen-Dazs | | | 哈根达斯 |
| Vanilla Swiss Almond | | | 香草瑞士杏仁 |
| Butter Pecan | | | 奶油核果 |
| Dulce de Leche | | | 牛奶太妃 |
| Frozen Yogurt | | | 酸奶冰激凌 |
| Sorbet | /ˈsɔːbət/ | n. | 果汁冰糕，冰冻果子露 |

## Exercises

*Directions: Decide whether the following statements are true (T) or false (F) according to the information in the passage.*

1. Häagen-Dazs has a history of more than one hundred years. ( )
2. Super-premium is the main feature of Häagen-Dazs. ( )
3. Häagen-Dazs, which is regarded as the representative of super-premium, now came from family workshop. ( )
4. Häagen-Dazs started out with a variety of flavors. ( )
5. Today Häagen-Dazs remains committed to developing new flavors. ( )
6. The family business prospered only after the innovation of new brand Häagen-Dazs. ( )
7. In the past 30 years, Häagen-Dazs has become a global phenomenon. You can buy it in 50 countries. ( )

*Directions: Guess the meanings of the words and phrases in the box according to the passage. Then, use them to complete the following sentences, changing the form if necessary.*

| insist on | prosper | throughout | start out |
| regard as | to name just a few | release from | |

1. She _____ his wearing a suit.
2. The museum is open daily _____ the year.
3. Capital punishment _____ inhuman and immoral.
4. Flowers available include roses, tulips and lilies, _____.
5. She _____ on her legal career in 1990.
6. Fire fighters took 2 hours to _____ the driver _____ the wreckage (汽车残骸).
7. The economy _____ under his administration.

*Directions: Pay attention to different parts of speech and select the appropriate word to fill in the blanks.*

1. noisy   noise   voice   sound
   a. Don't make so much _____.
   b. She could hear the _____ of children laughing.
   c. The engine is very _____ at high speed.
   d. Keep your _____ down.
2. super   superior   superiority
   a. I had a _____ time in Italy.
   b. The enemy won because of their _____ number.
   c. I prefer the _____ of this operating system.

3. prosper    prosperity    prosperous
   a. His business _____.
   b. The country is enjoying a period of peace and _____.
   c. Farmers are more _____ in the south of the country.
4. except    exception    exceptional    exceptionally
   a. We work every day _____ Sunday.
   b. Most of the buildings in the town are modern, but the church is an _____.
   c. At the age of five he showed _____ talent as a musician.
   d. The weather, even for January, was _____ cold.

*Directions: First translate the following English sentences into Chinese Then, pay attention to the italicized (斜体的) parts in the English sentences and translate the Chinese sentences by simulating the structure of the English sentences.*

1. To produce the finest ice cream, he *insisted on* using only the finest, purest ingredient.
   他们执意演奏他们的音乐直到深夜。
2. *Since then*, it has become a global phenomenon and it can be bought in 50 countries.
   自那以后，我们还没有他的音讯。
3. To this day, Häagen-Dazs *remains committed to* developing exceptional new super premium frozen dessert experiences, releasing new flavors every year.
   政府承诺要改革卫生保健制度。
4. Since the beginning, Häagen-Dazs has tried to bring new frozen dessert experiences to its customers, including special flavors such as Vanilla Swiss Almond, Butter Pecan and Dulce de Leche, *to name just a few*.
   这间公寓配套齐全，有各种家用电器，举几个例子如：空调、微波炉和洗衣机。

*Directions: Group activity.*

Work in group to introduce the most popular food in your hometown. If possible, introduce the food production methods and history.

## Part IV  Grammar

## 形容词和副词

**一、形容词的基本用法：**
形容词修饰名词,说明事物或人的性质或特征。通常,可将形容词分成性质形容词和叙述形容词两类,其位置不一定都放在名词前面。

1) 直接说明事物的性质或特征的形容词是性质形容词,它有级的变化,可以用程度副词修饰,在句中可作定语、表语和补语。如：hot 热的。

2) 叙述形容词只能作表语,所以又称为表语形容词。这类形容词没有级的变化,也不可用程度副词修饰。大多数以 a 开头的形容词都属于这一类。如：afraid 害怕的。

（错） He is an ill man.　　　（对） The man is ill.
（错） She is an afraid girl.　　（对） The girl is afraid.

3) 形容词作定语修饰名词时,要放在名词的前边。但是如果形容词修饰以 -thing 为字尾的词语时,要放在这些词之后,例如：something nice

### 形容词的比较级和最高级的变化

**1. 规则变化**

| 情况 | 构成法 | 原级 | 比较级 | 最高级 |
| --- | --- | --- | --- | --- |
| 单音节词和少数双音节词 | 一般在词尾加-er,或者加 -est | tall<br>long | taller<br>longer | tallest<br>longest |
| 以字母 e 结尾 | 加 -r 或者 -st | fine<br>nice | finer<br>nicer | finest<br>nicest |
| 重读闭音节词只有一个辅音字母 | 先双写辅音字母,再加-er 或 -est | big<br>hot | bigger<br>hotter | biggest<br>hottest |
| 以辅音字母+y 结尾的双音节词 | 先改 y 为 i,再加 -er 或 -est | easy<br>happy | easier<br>happier | easiest<br>happiest |
| 多音节词和部分双音节词 | 其前加 more 或 most | popular<br>beautiful | more popular<br>more beautiful | most popular<br>most beautiful |

**2. 不规则变化,如：**

good → better → best　　　　many/much → more → most
far → farther/further → farthest/furthest

## 二、副词的基本用法

副词主要用来修饰动词,形容词,副词或其他结构。

**(一)副词的位置:**

1) 在动词之前。

2) 在 be 动词、助动词之后。

3) 多个助动词时,副词一般放在第一个助动词后。

**注意:**

a. 大多数方式副词位于句尾,但宾语过长,副词可以提前,以使句子平衡。

　　We could see very clearly a strange light ahead of us.

b. 方式副词 well, badly (糟、坏), hard 等只放在句尾。

　　He speaks English well.

**(二)副词的排列顺序:**

1) 时间,地点副词,小单位的在前,大单位在后。

2) 方式副词,短的在前,长的在后,并用 and 或 but 等连词连接。

　　Please write slowly and carefully.

3) 多个不同副词排列:程度+地点+方式+时间副词。

**注意:** 副词 very 可以修饰修饰词,但不能修饰动词。

改错:(错)　I very like English.

　　　(对)　I like English very much.

**注意:** 副词 enough 要放在修饰词的后面,形容词 enough 放在名词前后都可。

I don't know him well enough.

There is enough food for everyone to eat.

There is food enough for everyone to eat.


### 副词的比较级和最高级的变化

**1. 规则变化**

| 情况 | 构成法 | 原级 | 比较级 | 最高级 |
| --- | --- | --- | --- | --- |
| 单音节词和少数双音节词 | 一般在词尾加-er,或者加 – est | hard<br>fast | harder<br>faster | hardest<br>fastest |
| 以字母 e 结尾 | 加 – r 或者 – st | fine<br>late | finer<br>later | finest<br>latest |
| 重读闭音节词只有一个辅音字母 | 先双写辅音字母,再加-er 或 – est | big | bigger | biggest |
| 以辅音字母 + y 结尾的双音节词 | 先改 y 为 i,再加 – er 或- est | early<br>wisely | earlier<br>wiselier | earliest<br>wiseliest |
| 多音节词和部分双音节词 | 其前加 more 或 most | often<br>easily | more often<br>more easily | most often<br>most easily |

## 2. 不规则变化,如：

well→better→best　　　badly→worse→worst　　　much→more→most

far→further→furthest　　little→less→least

## Exercises

*Directions: There are 10 incomplete statements here. You are required to complete each statement by choosing the appropriate answer from the 4 choices marked A, B, C, D.*

1. Being healthy is more important _____ being rich.
   A. so　　　　　　　　B. than　　　　　　　C. rather　　　　　　D. as
2. This film is _____ interesting as that one.
   A. as　　　　　　　　B. so　　　　　　　　C. that　　　　　　　D. which
3. It was very hot yesterday, but it is _____ today.
   A. even hotter　　　　　　　　　　　　　　B. more hotter
   C. much more hot　　　　　　　　　　　　D. much hot
4. These children are _____ this year than they were last year.
   A. more tall　　　　　B. more taller　　　　C. very taller　　　　D. much taller
5. Hainan is a very large island. It's the second _____ island in China.
   A. large　　　　　　　B. larger　　　　　　C. largest　　　　　　D. most large
6. The population of Shandong is _____ than that of Sichuan.
   A. smaller　　　　　　B. larger　　　　　　C. less　　　　　　　D. large
7. Which is _____, the sun, the moon or the earth?
   A. bigger　　　　　　B. biggest　　　　　　C. the biggest　　　　D. larger
8. This necklace looks _____ and sells _____ .
   A. well, well　　　　　B. good, nice　　　　C. nice, good　　　　D. nice, well
9. China has a large population than _____ in the world.
   A. all the countries　　B. every country　　　C. any country　　　　D. any other country
10. Mary says this is the _____ decision she has ever made in her career life.
    A. bad　　　　　　　B. badly　　　　　　C. worse　　　　　　D. worst

*Directions: Fill in each blank with the proper form of the words given in the brackets.*

1. The _____ (careful) the proposal is considered, the worse it appears.
2. As Edison grew _____ (old) , he never lost his interest in science.
3. John is the _____ (clever) student I have ever taught.
4. I want to rent a new apartment that is _____ (comfortable) than this one.
5. Singapore is _____ (far) away from the South Pole than from the North Pole.

## Part V  Applied Writing

### Notes (便条)

便条是一种简单的书信,多用于比较熟悉的同学、同事和亲友之间的一种应用文。主要目的是为了尽快地把最新的信息、通知、要求或者活动的时间、地点转告给对方。便条内容和类型不尽相同,可以灵活变通。但各类便条必须包括以下几个基本要素;1) Date:便条日期 2) Salutation:称呼 3) Body:正文 4)Signature:署名。

**写作注意事项:**

1. 便条实际上是一种简易书信,谈的都是当天或三两天内的事。时间常常不写年月,只写日期或上下午,或几点钟。
2. 便条一般是临时通知、询问事宜,往往是托人转交或在某一场合的直接留言,不需要邮寄,所以不用信封。
3. 写便条时要求开门见山、三言两语把意思表达清楚,句式简单、用词随便,接近口语。
4. 如果把假条或留言条装在信封里请别人转交,"转交"一词,英文一般用"care of",但信封上多用缩写式:c / o。如:班长收,烦请李平转交。应写为:

Monitor

c / o Li Ping

### Sample1: Appointments

Feb.10

Helen,
    Could we see each other for about an hour on Friday afternoon at 2 o'clock?

Xiaoming

### Sample2: Apologies

Oct.9

Susan,
    I am sorry to have to tell you that I shall not be able to come to the party, because I have a bad cold. I do hope you will have a good time.

Feifei

## Sample3: Informal invitations

3rd July

Dear Ms. Gates,

We are having a party in our classroom, # 302, to celebrate.... Would it be possible for you to join us on Friday, December 27, at 7 p.m.? We would be very happy if you could be with us.

Students of Class3 Grade1

## Sample4: Request

Jan. 10th

Dear Mr. Jiang,

I am terribly sorry that I shall be unable to attend this morning two periods of English Class due to a bad cold and high fever. Enclosed is a certificate from the doctor who said I must stay in bed for a few days. I will go back to school as soon as I recover.

Your kind permission will be greatly appreciated.

Your student,
Wang Ping

## Sample5: Thanks

Dear Mr. Smith,

I am writing to tell you how grateful I am for your warm hospitality during my stay in New York. I enjoyed it greatly.

Fang Tao

## Sample6: Messages

Dear Mr. White,

Here is a ticket for the exhibition tomorrow. The car will come around at 10:00 tomorrow morning.

Mary

## Exercises

*Directions: This part is to test your ability to do practical writing.*

**说 明：**

1. 以李超的名义给胡老师写一张请假条。假条内容：在一次交通事故中左腿受伤，医生要求他卧床休息一周。希望老师准假一周，日期是5月21日。
2. 江飞给朋友李明留言。内容：春节临近，特邀几位好友晚上5点在丽江酒店6号包间小聚。
3. Tom留言给Bob，因为下午3点要去机场接朋友，要求改到明天上午10点讨论事情。如果不行，请电话联系再改约时间。

## Part VI  Cultural Express

### Pizza Hut

Pizza Hut is an American restaurant chain and international franchise that offers different styles of pizza along with side dishes including salad, pasta (意大利通心粉), buffalo wings (布法罗鸡翅), breadsticks, and garlic bread.

Pizza Hut is split into several different restaurant formats: the original family-style dine-in locations; store front delivery and carry-out locations; and hybrid locations that offer carry-out, delivery, and dine-in options. Many full-size Pizza Hut locations offer lunch buffet (自助午餐), with "all-you-can-eat" pizza, salad, bread sticks, and a special pasta.

Vintage "Red Roof" locations can be found throughout the United States, and quite a few exist in the UK and Australia. Even so, many such locations offer delivery/carryout service. This building style was common in the late 1960s and early 1970s. The name "Red Roof" is somewhat anachronistic now, since many locations have brown roofs. Dozens of "Red Roofs" have closed or been rebuilt. Many "Red Roof" branches have beer if not a full bar, music from a jukebox, and sometimes an arcade. In the mid 1980s, the company moved into other successful formats including delivery/carryout and the fast food "Express" model.

The oldest continuously operating Pizza Hut in the world is in Manhattan, Kansas, in a shopping and tavern district known as Aggieville near Kansas State University.

Pizza Hut's prototype version of a restaurant (1958—1961) starts at Wichita State University. This was only used at four prototype Pizza Hut locations. There are only a few menu items on this version. Pizza Hut was founded in 1958 by brothers Dan and Frank Carney in their hometown of Wichita, Kansas. When a friend suggested opening a pizza parlor, they agreed that the idea could prove successful, and they borrowed $600 from their mother to start a business with partner John Bender. Renting a small building at 503 South Bluff in downtown Wichita and purchasing secondhand equipment to make pizzas, the Carneys and Bender opened the first "Pizza Hut" restaurant; on opening night, they gave pizza away to encourage community interest. They chose the name "Pizza Hut" since the sign they purchased only had enough space for nine characters and spaces. Additional restaurants were opened, with the first franchise unit opening in 1959 in Topeka, Kansas. The original Pizza Hut building was later relocated to the Wichita State University campus.

Dan and Frank Carney soon decided that they needed to have a good standard image. The Carney brothers contacted Wichita architect Richard D. Burke, who designed the distinctive mansard roof shape (折线形屋顶) and standardized layout, hoping to counter competition from Shakey's Pizza (喜客比萨), a chain that was expanding on the west coast. The franchise network continued to grow through friends and business associates, and by 1964 a unique standardized building appearance and layout was established for franchised and company-owned stores, creating a universal look that customers easily recognized.

By 1972, with 314 stores nationwide, Pizza Hut went public on the New York Stock Exchange (纽约证券交易所) under the stock ticker symbol NYSE: PIZ. In 1978, Pizza Hut was acquired by PepsiCo (百事公司), who later also bought KFC and Taco Bell (塔可钟墨西哥快餐厅). In 1997, the three restaurant chains were spun off into Tricon, and in 2001 joined with Long John Silver's and A&W Restaurants to become Yum! Brands (百胜餐饮).

## 拓展词汇

### 西餐

aperitif 饭前酒；dim sum 点心；fires 炸薯条；baked potato 烤马铃薯；mashed potatoes 马铃薯泥；omelette 煎蛋；pudding 布丁；pastries 点心；crab meat 蟹肉；prawn 明虾；braised beef 炖牛肉；bacon 熏肉；fried egg 煎蛋；scramble egg 炒蛋

### 中式早餐

clay oven rolls 烧饼；fried bread stick 油条；boiled dumplings 水饺；steamed bread 馒头；rice and vegetable roll 饭团；salted duck egg 咸鸭蛋；soybean milk 豆浆

### 中式菜名

sweet-and-sour pork with pineapple 菠萝香酥肉；steamed spareribs with rice flower 粉蒸排骨；sweet-and-sour pork 古老肉；stewed meatballs with brown sauce 红烧狮子头；braised meat 扣肉；steamed pork with rice flower 米粉蒸肉；roast duck 烤鸭；beggar's chicken 叫花鸡；steamed Nanjing duck 南京板鸭；wined chicken 醉鸡；smoked duck 樟茶鸭；instant-boiled mutton 涮羊肉

### 面类

sliced noodles 刀削面；spicy hot noodles 麻辣面；seafood noodles 乌龙面；flat noodles 板条；pork , pickled mustard green noodles 榨菜肉丝面；rice noodles 米粉

### 汤类

seaweed soup 紫菜汤；oyster soup 牡蛎汤；egg & vegetable soup 蛋花汤；fish ball soup 鱼丸汤

# Unit 5

## Movie

*Learning Objectives:*

You are able to:

☞ Identify some basic sounds of letters

☞ Use the proper expressions to comment on movies

☞ Know the use of verb

☞ Write memos

You are suggested to:

☞ Be familiar with some famous movie culture

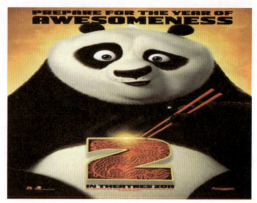

    Movie is considered to be an important art form, a source of popular entertainment and a powerful method for educating people. Some movies have become popular with a huge number of fans worldwide. Besides, the making and showing of movies is a source of profit. In the United States today, much of the film industry is centered around Hollywood, where the Academy Awards (also known as "the Oscars") is held each year to give recognition to successful films.

## Part I  Phonetics

### Task 1  Identifying Their Pronunciations

*Directions: Listen to the following words and read after the speaker, paying attention to the colored parts.*

| /w/ | /j/ | |
| /m/ | /n/ | /ŋ/ |
| /ts/ | /dz/ | /l/ |

| | | | | |
|---|---|---|---|---|
| (1) what | we | week | white | wind |
| (2) your | yellow | yummy | year | young |
| (3) map | name | trumpet | tomato | more |
| (4) no | not | soon | many | number |
| (5) long | ring | English | length | morning |
| (6) eats | hurts | parents | cats | rabbits |
| (7) beds | friends | finds | birds | needs |
| (8) look | light | lock | luck | laugh |
| (9) tall | old | meal | middle | well |

• Unit 5  Movie •

*Practice: Write down the sound of the underlined part of the words.*

| wi<u>n</u>dow | si<u>ng</u> | dru<u>m</u> | smi<u>le</u> | <u>l</u>ake |
|---|---|---|---|---|
| _____ | _____ | _____ | _____ | _____ |

## Task 2   Appreciating a Poem

*Directions: Listen to the poem written by William Butler Yeats "When You Are Old". Choose the words you hear to fill in the blanks.*

| shadow | /ˈʃadəʊ/ | n. | 阴影,影子 |
| grace | /ɡreɪs/ | n. | 优美,风度,魅力 |
| beauty | /ˈbjuːti/ | n. | 美,美人,美的东西 |
| pilgrim | /ˈpɪlɡrɪm/ | n. | 香客,朝圣者 |
| sorrow | /ˈsɒrəʊ/ | n. | 悲痛,悲伤,遗憾,懊悔,<br>不幸的事,忧患 |
| bend | /bend/ | v. | (使)弯曲,屈身 |
| murmur | /ˈməːmə/ | v. | 小声说,私下低声抱怨 |

### Poem    When You Are Old

*William Butler Yeats*

When you are old and gray and _____ (full, fall) of sleep,
And nodding by the _____ (fair, fire), take down this book,
And slowly _____ (read, rid) and dream of the soft look
Your eyes had once, and of their shadows _____ (dip, deep);
How many loved your moments of glad grace,
And loved your beauty with love _____ (false, force) or true,
But one man loved the pilgrim _____ (soul, so) in you,
And loved the sorrows of your changing face;
And bending down beside the glowing bars,
Murmur, a little sadly, how Love _____ (fled, flex),
And paced upon the mountains overhead,
And _____ (hit, hid) his face amid a crowd of stars.

### Task 3   Time for Fun: Tongue Twister

*Directions: Practice the tongue twister sentence by sentence after the speaker. Pay attention to the sounds.*

(1) Can you can a can as a canner can a can?

(2) The man with fair hair dare not repair their chairs there because there is a bear there.

(3) Peter Piper picked a peck of pickled peppers. A peck of pickled peppers Peter Piper picked. If Peter Piper picked a peck of pickled peppers, where's the peck of pickled peppers Peter Piper picked?

## Part II   Listening and Speaking

### Task 1   Short Dialogues

*Directions: Listen to the following short dialogues and fill in the blanks with the information you get from the recording. Each dialogue will be read twice.*

(1) **W:** Can you tell me where the ChangJiang _____ is?
   **M:** I'm on my way there myself, so I'll _____ you.

(2) **W:** What's on TV _____?
   **M:** I don't think there's anything _____.
   **W:** Then why not go to the _____?
   **M:** That sounds great.

(3) **W:** Do you like Kevin Costner. I like his _____.
       He is the _____ role in *Dances with Wolves*.
   **M:** Yes, I like him, too. The supporting actor is Morgan Freeman. I've heard that he _____ the best supporting actor on the _____ Oscar.

(4) **W:** Can I _____ you?
   **M:** I'd like to buy two _____ for "Avatar". How much are they?
   **W:** _____ dollars.
   **M:** Ok, here you are.

(5) **W:** Excuse me, could you tell us what's _____ tonight?
   **M:** *Dances with Wolves.*
   **W:** Is it an _____ movie?
   **M:** Well, sort of. There's a lot of action, but I'd rather call it a _____.

## Task 2    Answering the Questions

*Directions: You will hear 5 recorded questions. Listen carefully and choose the proper answer to each question. The questions will be read twice.*

(1) A. He was caught in the rain and has caught a bad cold.
    B. He didn't want to leave because of catching a cold.
    C. He failed to catch the plane because of the rain.
    D. He had a bad cold and missed the plane.

(2) A. He is an expert in IT.
    B. He is interested in IT.
    C. He often does research on IT with us.
    D. He likes IT very much.

(3) A. Do more speaking.
    B. Remember more words.
    C. Improve his spoken English.
    D. Do more listening.

(4) A. Because he has difficulty understanding the timetable of the bus service.
    B. Because he doesn't know where to take the bus.
    C. Because he wants to make sure if he can catch the 3:00 bus.
    D. Because he doesn't know when to take the bus.

(5) A. She is now studying MBA abroad.    B. She may take other courses.
    C. She is getting on well with her study.    D. She has finished MBA course.

## Task 3    Oral Practice

*Warm-Up 1: Match the expressions in the left column with the expressions in the right column so as to form 7 short dialogues.*

| | |
|---|---|
| (1) —What can I do for you? | —Yes. I would like to know the showing day for the film "Avatar". |
| (2) —How many tickets do you need? | —Sean Connery's 007. |
| (3) —How much is one ticket? | —At 7:00 p.m.. |
| (4) —What time will the movie start? | —Yes, I like Zhang Ziyi. |
| (5) —What's on the Peace Theatre? | —20 yuan each. |
| (6) —What do you think of the film? | —Exciting. |
| (7) —Do you know any movie stars? | —Two, please. |

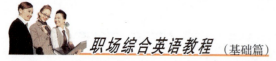

*Warm-Up 2: Work with your partner to praltise the following useful expressions.*

**If you are a salesman / saleswoman in a theater, you can say**

(1) Is there anything I can do for you?

(2) How many tickets do you need?

(3) What movie do you want to see?

**If you are a customer, you can say**

(1) Excuse me, what is the movie tonight?

(2) Could you please give me two tickets for *Flowers Of War* (《金陵十三钗》)?

(3) I'd like to see ...

(4) How much is one ticket for this movie?

**Dialogue**

*George and Heather are friends. They are planning to see a movie.*

George:  Hi, Heather. I was wondering if you're free tomorrow night.

Heather: Well, George, I guess I am. Why do you ask?

George:  I was just given a pair of "Star Wars" movie tickets by a friend and was thinking of inviting you along for the opening premier. Are you interested?

Heather: Yeah, definitely. Thanks for inviting me.

George:  Well, let's see. The movie starts at 10 p.m.. We should get there at least 1 hour earlier because there'll be a big line. I could pick you up at your house at 8, if that's OK with you.

Heather: 8 o'clock? That's fine with me.

George:  Okay, good.

Heather: So I'll see you tomorrow at 8 then?

George:  Yeah. That's great. I'll see you tomorrow night, Heather.

Heather: Okay, George. Bye.

George:  Bye, Heather.

### New Words and Expressions

| opening premier | | | 首映式 |
|---|---|---|---|
| definitely | /ˈdɛfɪnɪtli/ | adv. | 确定地,一定地 |
| line | /lʌɪn/ | n. | 队伍,排队 |
| pick sb. up | | | 接某人 |

### Task 4   Role Play

(1) Imagine you are a clerk in a cinema. Now you are doing something for a *customer*. Make up a dialogue between them. The patterns you learned just now and the expressions given below may be of some help to you.

| Expressions | |
|---|---|
| Welcome to ABC Cinema. | 欢迎来到ABC电影院。 |
| Would you like to buy a ticket? | 你要买电影票吗？ |
| I want to know when...is showing. | 我想了解一下某某电影的播放时间。 |
| showing days | 播放天数 |
| How much is the ticket? | 票价多少？ |
| Here are your tickets. | 给您票。 |

(2) Now you and your friend Lily have come to a cinema. You want to buy tickets for a film. The cinema assistant serves you. Make up a dialogue according to the information. The patterns you learned just now and the expressions given below may be of some help to you.

| Expressions | | | |
|---|---|---|---|
| serve | /sə:v/ | v. | 服务，侍候 |
| What film would you like to watch? | | | 您想看什么电影？ |
| order | /'ɔ:də/ | v. | 订票 |

### Task 5   Leisure Time: Learning to Sing a Song

1. Listen to the song "My heart will go on".
2. Listen to the song again and fill in the missing words.

**My Heart Will Go On**

Every night in my _____
I see you I feel you
That is how I know you go on
Far across the _____ and _____ between us
You have come to show you go on
Near far wherever you are
I believe that the _____ does go on
Once more you opened the door

And you're here in my heart
And my heart will go on and on

You're here there's nothing I _____
And I know that my heart will go on
We'll stay forever this way
You are _____ in my heart
And my heart will go on and on

Love can touch us one time
And last for a _____
And never let go till we're _____
Love was when I loved you
One _____ time I hold you
In my life we'll always go on
Near far wherever you are
I believe that the heart does go on
Once more you opened the door
And you're here in my heart
And my heart will go on and on

3. Learn to sing the song after the singer.

## Part III  Reading

### Text A

### Wizard Series Ends

Who could have anticipated that the child fans of the *original* story about an 11-year-old boy wizard would *loyally* follow the series well into their 20s?

That's the *magic* of the Harry Potter series. Now, with the release of the final *installment*, *Harry Potter and the Deathly Hallows: Part 1*, fans must accept that the series is nearing its end.

Which is the final installment of Harry Potter series for the time being? It's *doubtful* that popular culture will see anything quite like the Harry Potter phenomenon for a long time to come. Harry Potter's *impact* has unquestionably been felt in both book sales and box office receipts. But why has the series been so successful?

"The *genius* of JK Rowling was that she *grounded* the wish *fulfillment* of a real kid with magical powers in the context of the real world. You enter the *fantasy* with her," Lionel Wigram, a production executive at Warner Bros, told the Los Angeles Times.

And, after 10 years, millions of fans seem to have enjoyed the ride. "It's a fantasy that's also very true to life," said Deng Hao, 22, a junior student at Shandong University who's also a Harry Potter fan. "The special effects in the movies don't

outweigh the fact that it's deeply personal," said Deng. "It's really about the characters." Jemima Owen, a 20-year-old college student in the UK, was in her final year of primary school when the first Harry Potter film was released. She recently wrote an article for The Observer from a fan's perspective. "Eleven-year-olds picking up the first Harry Potter book now will never understand the anticipation and yearning we felt as we waited three years for the release of the next installment," she wrote. "To say we 'grew up' with Harry, Ron and Hermione might be clichéd, but to me, the end of the series is like a farewell to childhood."

(*21st Century* November 17, 2001)

### New Words

| | | | |
|---|---|---|---|
| wizard | /ˈwɪzəd/ | n. | 男巫,怪才 |
| ★ original | /əˈrɪdʒɪn(ə)l, ɒ-/ | adj. | 起初的,原作的 |
| loyally | /ˈlɔɪəli/ | adv. | 忠实地 |
| ★ magic | /ˈmædʒɪk/ | n. | 魔力 |
| ★ installment | /ɪnˈstɔːlm(ə)nt/ | n. | 部分 |
| doubtful | /ˈdaʊtfʊl, -f(ə)l/ | adj. | 怀疑的 |
| impact | /ˈɪmpakt/ | n. | 影响 |
| ★ genius | /ˈdʒiːnɪəs/ | n. | 才华 |
| ground | /ɡraʊnd/ | v. | 为……提供背景 |
| ☆ fulfillment | /fʊlˈfɪlm(ə)nt/ | n. | 实现 |
| fantasy | /ˈfantəsi, -zi/ | n. | 魔幻世界 |
| ☆ outweigh | /aʊtˈweɪ/ | v. | 在重要性或价值方面超过 |
| character | /ˈkarəktə/ | n. | 角色,人物 |
| ☆ perspective | /pəˈspɛktɪv/ | n. | 角度 |
| yearning | /ˈjɜːnɪŋ/ | n. | 思念,渴望 |
| ☆ clichéd | /ˈkliːʃeɪd/ | adj. | 陈词滥调的 |
| farewell | /fɛːˈwɛl/ | n. | 告别,再见 |

### Phrases and Expressions

| | |
|---|---|
| for the time being | 目前,暂时 |
| production executive | 执行制片人 |
| millions of | 好几百万 |
| from a ... perspective | 从……角度 |
| pick up | 拿起,捡起 |
| a farewell to childhood | 告别童年 |

| **Proper Names** | |
|---|---|
| Harry Potter | 哈利·波特 |
| Harry Potter and the Deathly Hallows: Part 1 | 哈利·波特与死亡圣器(上) |
| Warner Bros | 华纳兄弟公司 |
| Los Angeles Times | 洛杉矶时报 |

## Exercises

*Directions: Answer the following questions according to the passage.*

1. How long has Harry Potter been followed?
2. What was the genius of JK Rowling?
3. How has the impact of Harry Potter been felt?
4. Who is Deng Hao? What are his opinions on Harry Potter?
5. Who is Jemima Owen? How did Jemima Owen feel about Harry Potter?

*Directions: Choose the best meaning of each italicized word according to the context and try to tell how you get the answer.*

1. Harry Potter's impact has unquestionably been felt in both book sales and *box office receipts*.
   A. 办公收据   B. 票房收入
   C. 窗口收益

2. Eleven-year-olds picking up the first Harry Potter book now will never understand the *anticipation and yearning.* we felt as we waited three years for the release of the next installment.
   A. 期待和渴望   B. 预计和思念
   C. 想象和渴望

3. The end of the *series* is like a farewell to childhood.
   A. 连续   B. 次序   C. 系列

4. To say we 'grew up' with Harry, Ron and Hermione might be *clichéd*.
   A. 陈腐的   B. 铅板   C. 陈词滥调

5. The special effects in the movies don't *outweigh* the fact that it's deeply personal.
   A. 超重   B. 超过   C. 比……重

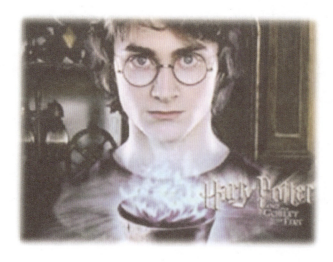

Unit 5  Movie

## Vocabulary

Directions: Match each word in Column A with its definition in Column B

| Column A | Column B |
| --- | --- |
| 1. anticipate | a. a magic world which is completely unrelated to reality |
| 2. release | b. the action of saying goodbye |
| 3. doubtful | c. to be more important or valuable than something else |
| 4. ground | d. a way of thinking about something |
| 5. fantasy | e. to make a CD, video, film etc. available for people to buy or see |
| 6. perspective | f. a person in a book, play, film etc. |
| 7. farewell | g. faithfully |
| 8. outweigh | h. not sure whether something is true or right |
| 9. loyally | i. to be based on something |
| 10. character | j. to expect that something will happen and be ready for it |

Directions: Complete the following sentences with words from Column A above. Change the form where necessary.

1. People gathered at the square to give _____ to the victims of the earthquake.
2. Your children sometimes can't distinguish between _____ and reality.
3. The benefits of the plan _____ the disadvantages
4. His father's death gave him a whole new _____ on life.
5. When will the latest Harry Potter movie _____?
6. Candida is the most interesting _____ in the play.
7. He has always _____ defended his country.
8. I'm still _____ whether I should accept the job.
9. Lewis's ideas were _____ in his Christian faith.
10. A good speaker is able to _____ an audience's needs and concerns.

Directions: Translate the following sentences into English.

1. The film _____
   (最近才上映的).
2. He _____
   (得到了那本书) in a most unlikely place.
3. The cat _____
   (跟随她到了厨房).
4. _____ (难以确定) whether the old man will recover from the operation.
5. You should _____
   (根据事实发表意见).

107

Text B

## I'd Like to Thank My Mother ...
*Trina Del Vecchio*

Accepting an award may seem like a simple task, but each year the Academy Awards proves there may be more to it than you might think. So the question remains: what makes a great acceptance speech? Here are three tips to keep in mind for your next shining occasion:

1. Be grateful and humble.

Make sure you thank the important people who helped you reach your goal. It's only natural to be a little emotional, so use this to inspire and personally relate to the audience. At this year's Oscars, *The King's Speech* director Tom Hooper told the story of how he only came to make the movie thanks to the help of his Australian mother, who was in the audience. He showed grace and humility when he mentioned her: "So, with this tonight, I honor you and the moral of the story is, listen to your mother."

2. Keep it short.

Say as much as you can in as few words as possible. There's no need to thank every single person you know. As Oscar producer Bruce Cohen warned contenders at the annual nominees luncheon before this year's show, "Nothing is more deadly than a winner reading a list of names." Make each sentence meaningful and don't get too carried away.

3. Finally, maximize your moment.

Don't be afraid to have a little fun and say something memorable. Clever wit and humor will help your speech stand out in a good way and keep everyone entertained. Don't make rude and inappropriate jokes, especially about others. Such jokes may get everyone talking, but you may be the only one laughing in the end. This time, Melissa Leo's use of the F-word during her acceptance speech was the first in Oscar history. She said it before covering her mouth: "I really don't mean to offend."

# Unit 5  Movie

## New Words

| | | | |
|---|---|---|---|
| award | /əˈwɔːd/ | n. | 奖项 |
| grateful | /ˈgreɪtfʊl, -f(ə)l/ | adj. | 感恩的 |
| ★ humble | /ˈhʌmb(ə)l/ | adj. | 谦逊的 |
| goal | /gəʊl/ | n. | 目标 |
| emotional | /ɪˈməʊʃ(ə)n(ə)l/ | adj. | 情感的 |
| director | /dɪˈrεktə, dʌɪ-/ | n. | 导演 |
| grace | /greɪs/ | n. | 风度 |
| ☆ humility | /hjʊˈmɪlɪti/ | n. | 谦虚 |
| ★ moral | /ˈmɒr(ə)l/ | n. | 寓意 |
| producer | /prəˈdjuːsə/ | n. | 制片人 |
| ☆ contender | /kənˈtεnd/ | n. | 竞争者 |
| show | /ʃəʊ/ | n. | (电视或广播)节目 |
| ★ maximize | /ˈmaksɪmʌɪz/ | v. | 最大化 |
| ★ wit | /wɪt/ | n. | 才智,智慧 |
| humor | /ˈhjuːmə/ | n. | 幽默 |
| ☆ inappropriate | /ɪnəˈprəʊprɪət/ | adj. | 不适宜的 |
| offend | /əˈfεnd/ | v. | 冒犯 |

## Phrases and Expressions

| | |
|---|---|
| seem like | 好像,似乎,看来 |
| keep in mind | 记住 |
| make sure | 确保,设法保证 |
| relate to | 涉及,与……相关 |
| thanks to | 幸亏,多亏,由于 |
| nominees luncheon | 提名者午宴 |
| be/get carried away | 失去理智 |
| stand out | 脱颖而出 |
| F-word | 粗话 |

## Proper Names

| | | | |
|---|---|---|---|
| Academy Awards | | | 奥斯卡金像奖 |
| Oscar | /ˈɔskə/ | n. | 奥斯卡 |
| Tom Hooper | | | 汤姆·胡珀 |
| Bruce Cohen | | | 布鲁斯·科恩 |
| Melissa Leo | | | 梅丽莎·莱昂 |

# Exercises

*Directions: Decide whether the following statements are true (T) or false (F) according to the information in the passage.*

1. Accepting an award may be a simple task, but each year the Academy Awards proves there may be more to it than you might think.  ( )
2. Accepting an award, you should be grateful and humble.  ( )
3. Tom Hooper showed grace and humility to say thanks to his mother.  ( )
4. Make each sentence short and don't get too carried away.  ( )
5. Maximize your moment by saying something memorable and having a little fun.  ( )
6. Don't make rude and inappropriate jokes, but you can tell some jokes about others.  ( )

*Directions: Guess the meanings of the words and phrases in the box according to the passage. Then, use them to complete the following sentences, changing the form if necessary.*

| thanks to | grateful | keep in mind | stand out |
| maximize | be/get carried away | entertain | relate to |

1. I am extremely _____ to all the teachers for their help.
2. _____ the window to full screen.
3. He _____ us for hours with his stories and jokes.
4. It's well to _____ that listening and speaking are as important as reading and writing in learning a language.
5. The passage _____ the situation in England.
6. I _____ and started shouting at the boss.
7. She's the sort of person who _____ in a crowd.
8. It was all a great success — _____ a lot of hard work.

*Directions: Pay attention to different parts of speech and select the appropriate word to fill in the blanks.*

1. dead   deadly   death   die
   a. My grandfather is _____, he _____ in 1980.
   b. They are _____ enemies.
   c. He looked _____ pale.
   d. Do you believe in life after _____.
2. offence   offend   offender   offending   offensive
   a. They'll be _____ if you don't go to their wedding.
   b. When it comes to pollution, the chemical industry is a major _____.

c. The photo on the cover of the book may cause _____ to some people.

d. The _____ driver received a large fine.

e. His comments were deeply _____ to a large number of single mothers.

3. meaning   meaningful   meaningless   means

a. She gave me a _____ look.

b. Fines are _____ to a huge company like that.

c. Her life seemed to have lost all _____.

d. Is there any _____ of contacting him?

4. nature   natural   naturally   naturalness

a. After a while, we _____ started talking about the children.

b. The _____ of the dialogue made the book so true to life.

c. My hair soon grew back to its _____ colour.

d. Just let _____ take its course.

*Directions: First translate the following English sentences into Chinese. Then, pay attention to the italicized parts in the English sentences and translate the Chinese sentences by simulating the structure of the English ones.*

1. Accepting an award may *seem like* a simple task, but each year the Academy Award proves there may be more to it than you might think.
   当时这主意好像不错。

2. *Make sure* you thank the important people who helped you reach your goal.
   绝对不要让任何人发觉这件事。

3. The director told the story of how he only came to make the movie *thanks to the help of* his Australian mother, *who* was in the audience.
   多亏了在北京的朋友帮忙,他在酒店找到一份工作。

4. Don't be afraid to have a little fun and say *something memorable*.
   今天的报上有什么重要新闻吗?

5. Nothing is *more* deadly *than* a winner reading a list of names.
   她比她姐姐聪明多了。

6. Don't make rude and inappropriate jokes, *especially* about others.
   我喜爱罗马,尤其是春天的罗马。

7. Say as much as you can in *as* few words *as possible*.
   我们将会把你的订货尽早送到。

8. *There is no need to* thank every single person you know.
   你明天不必早起。

*Directions: Group activity.*

Discuss your favorite movie and present your reasons with reference to the following words.

| | | | |
|---|---|---|---|
| animated movie | science fiction movie | action movie | horror films |
| comedies | love stories | drama | musicals |
| scary | nervous | scream | horror |
| relaxing | popular with kids | adventure | excellent |
| touching | imagination | fantasy | magic |
| entertaining | romantic | boring | |

## Part IV  Grammar

### 动词 I  动词的种类

**一、及物动词和不及物动词**

及物动词是其后可直接跟宾语,并且必须跟有宾语才能使其意义完整的动词。不及物动词是其本身意义已经完整,后面不必跟宾语的动词。如:

(1) book a ticket（book 为及物动词）

(2) Birds fly.（fly 为不及物动词）

(3) Listen to me, look at the picture（listen 和 look 为不及物动词）

及物动词和不及物动词的区别:一个动词后面如果可以接宾语就是及物动词,如果后面不可以接宾语就是不及物动词。在英语中绝大部分动词,既可以用做及物动词,也可以用做不及物动词。

## 二、连系动词

连系动词本身有词义,但不能单独用作谓语,后边必须跟表语,构成系表结构说明主语的状况、性质、特征等情况。

| 分类 | 连系动词举例 | 例句 |
| --- | --- | --- |
| 状态系动词 | 只有be一个 | He is a student. 他是一名学生。 |
| 持续系动词 | keep, rest, remain, stay, lie, stand | He always kept silent at meeting. 他开会时总保持沉默。 |
| 系表动词 | seem, appear, look | He looks happy. 他看起来很开心。 |
| 感官系动词 | feel, smell, sound, taste | This flower smells very sweet. 这朵花闻起来很香。 |
| 变化系动词 | become, grow, turn, fall, get, go, come, run | He became rich after that. 自那之后,他变富了。 |
| 终止系动词 | prove, turn out | The rumor proved false. 这谣言证实有假。 |

## 三、助动词和情态动词

助动词有 be,have,do,will(would),shall(should)。它们本身没有词义,只和实义动词的一定形式构成复合谓语,用来表示时态和语态,构成否定、疑问及加强语气等。如:

(1) —Do you like college life? 你喜欢大学生活吗?
　　—Yes, I like it very much. 是,我很喜欢。

(2) When shall we go home? 我们什么时候回家?

(3) Don't interrupt me! 别打扰我!

情态动词表示说话人的语气或情态。情态动词本身有词义,但不完全,不能单独作谓语,必须和不带to的动词不定式,即动词原形一起构成谓语,没有人称和数的变化。多数情态动词有过去式。

(1) —Can I have a look at your new pen? 我可以看一看你的新钢笔吗?
　　—Sure. 当然可以。

(2) —Must we hand in our exercise books now? 我们现在就要交练习本吗?
　　—No, you needn't. / No, you don't have to.
　　不必。(这种情况下,一般不用mustn't)

(3) Will you close the window? It's a bit cold. 请把窗户关上好吗? 有点冷。

(4) Would you like another glass of beer? 再来杯啤酒好吗?

(5) He might be ill. 他可能生病了。

## 四、短语动词

动词加副词或介词等构成的动词短语叫短语动词。短语动词的构成基本有下列几种:

1. 动词+副词,如:black out 熄灯,中断。
2. 动词+介词,如:look into 浏览,观察。
3. 动词+副词+介词,如:look forward to 期待,盼望。

## Part V  Applied Writing

### Memo (备忘录)

备忘录是一种录以备忘的公文,是一种简易公文。在公文函件中,它的等级是比较低的,主要用来提醒、督促对方,或就某个问题提出自己的意见或看法。在业务上,它一般用来补充正式文件的不足。通常用于公司内部传递信息,将实情、信息、观察资料等进行传阅,是公司内部最普通的书面交流形式。备忘录一般由to(收件人)、from(发件人)、subject(主题)、date(日期)、body(正文)组成。

【格式】

Memorandum/Memo(可以省略)

**To:**
**From:**
**Date:**
**Subject:**
_____
_____
_____
_____
_____(Body)

Sample:

**Memo**

**TO:** Henry Green, Sales Manager
**FROM:** Daniel Smith, Personnel Manager
**DATE:** May 4, 2012
**SUBJECT:** Applicants for Sales Post

　　Attached are the resumes and certificates of four applicants who have applied for your department position.
　　Please evaluate these applicants and then recommend people you want to interview to me. As soon as I have the names, I will make arrangement for the interviews.

Unit 5   Movie

### 写作注意事项：

1. 在 date, to, from, subject 字样后填上相应的内容。
2. 在上述字样下面空两行写正文。
3. 一般不用称呼和结尾礼词。
4. memo 这个词有时可以被省略，因为大多数 memo 都印在专门的公司用纸上。
5. 不必用过于复杂的单词，行文应该简洁，语言要有礼貌。

### Basic Expressions（常用表达）

◆ 说明备忘录的主要内容

☆ Below is the ... meeting/conference arrangement. 以下是……会议的安排。

☆ The following is a status update for ... 以下是……的最新状况。

◆ 布置任务

☆ I would like to receive (I would appreciate having) your reports/suggestions/proposals by Friday. 我期待周五能收到你的报告（提案）。

☆ Here is the arrangement. 安排如下。

◆ 说明附件内容

☆ Attached are the minutes for the meeting. 附上会议纪要。

☆ Some proposals are enclosed. 附上一些提议。

## Exercises

*Directions: This part is to test your ability to do practical writing. You are required to write a memo of about 100 words to the student service department and ask them to fix a telephone for each dormitory. Remember you do not have to translate the Chinese word for word.*

说明：李明向学生后勤处提出在学生宿舍安装电话的要求。说作为大学生他们需要和老师、朋友们联系，尽管有手机、电子邮件，但还是需要电话，希望后勤处能尽快解决这个问题。

```
                          MEMO

To: The leader of student service department
From: Li Ming
Date: August 16, 2012
Subject: Telephone
Dear Sir,
_____
_____
_____
_____
_____

Yours,
Li Ming
```

## Part VI  Cultural Express

### American "Panda" Movie Stirs Controversy

A Hollywood movie was met with an awkward situation last Saturday in China. While fans are standing in long queues to watch the first show, others are advocating a boycott on the American movie with Chinese story elements.

After "Kung Fu Panda"(《功夫熊猫》), a cartoon movie telling about a panda's Kung Fu master journey, hit China's silver screens in 2008, its sequel, Kung Fu Panda 2, was released in China just ahead of International Children's Day (国际儿童节), adding more Chinese elements such as shadow play (皮影戏) and lion dancing (舞狮). However, some Chinese artists and scholars argue that the movie, produced by

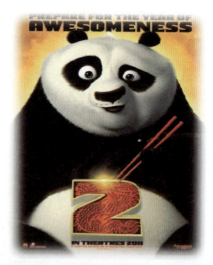

DreamWorks (梦工厂), has twisted Chinese culture and serves as a tool to "kidnap" the mind of the Chinese people. "Children's

Day should be pure. Don't turn it into a money-making day for Hollywood, and don't fool our next generation with American 'fast food'," according to an open letter to Chinese cinema managers written by Zhao Bandi, an avant-garde artist hoping to boycott the "Americanized" movie.

Over the past two weeks, Zhao has used his own money to pay to publish circulars in newspapers in Beijing and Guangzhou, urging fans not to watch the movie. "This is a battle," he said. In 2008, Zhao initiated similar campaigns to boycott Kung Fu Panda, which later set the country's cartoon box office record, selling tickets valued at 180 million yuan.

His move is backed by Kong Qingdong, a renowned professor of the Chinese language with the Peking University, who said Chinese elements have become advertising products to advocate American culture. "It is a cultural invasion," said Kong.

In the movie, the main character called "Po", a panda, is talkative, humorous, lovely and charmingly naive, and is widely believed to be a typical American figure.

However, the panda has won million of fans in China. On China's most popular microblog website, weibo.com, comments on the movie reached nearly 270 million entries. Most of the netizens post questions such as "Why can't we produce such brilliant movies ourselves?"

"I won't call it a cultural invasion," said Li Jiayi, a Beijing university student. "I see nothing bad for others to use our cultural elements to make a movie."

Yuan Weili, a girl in Shijiazhuang, capital of north China's Hebei Province, said at a cinema that she had been waiting three years to watch the sequel. "I'm a huge fan of Po. In spite of being a cartoon, it is still loved by many adults like me," said the 25-year-old after watching the first show at midnight.

Nine-year-old Zhang Miao watched with his parents. He made a Kung Fu pose and said, "I didn't see "Rio" (《里约大冒险》), and I'm not interested in pirates, but I gotta see Kong Fu Panda".

Cao Hui, deputy general manager (副总经理) with Shenzhen Global Digital Creations company (深圳全球数码制作公司), said instead of a "boycott", movie producers should learn from the movie to better make use of Chinese story elements. "Technically, Kung Fu Panda is not more advanced than Chinese movies, but as for story telling skills, Chinese movies have a long way to go," said Cao.

(**source:** http://news.xinhuanet.com/english2010/entertainment/2011-05/29)

## 拓展词汇

### 电影类型

documentary 文献片,纪录片;musical 音乐片;comedy 喜剧片;tragedy 悲剧片;detective movie 侦探片;literary film 文艺片;western movie 西部片;cartoon 卡通片;silent movie 无声片;dubbed film 译制片;disaster film 灾难片;newsreel 新闻片;trailer 预告片

### 电影演员

cast 演员阵容;film star/movie star 电影明星;actor 男电影演员;actress 女电影演员;stand-in 替身演员;stunt man 特技替身演员;extra 临时演员,特别客串

### 工作人员

producer 制片人;director 导演;assistant director 副导演;cameraman 摄影师;propsman 道具员;art director/set decorator 布景师;stagehand 化装师;lighting engineer 灯光师;film cutter 剪辑师;sound engineer/recording director 录音师;script girl 场记员;scenario writer/scenarist 剧作家;costumer 服装师

### 电影节

film festival 电影节;Academy Awards(Oscar)奥斯卡金像奖;Venice International Film Festival 威尼斯国际电影节;Cannes Film Festival 戛纳电影节;Berlin International Film Festival 柏林国际电影节

Unit 5　Movie

### 电影放映

distributer 发行人；premiere 首映式；first-run cinema 首轮影院；banned film 禁映影片；cencor's certificate 审查级别；A-certificate A 片（儿童不宜）；X-certificate 成人片；projection 放映

### 电影公司

Universal Pictures Corporation 环球电影公司；Warner Brothers 华纳电影公司；Pixar 皮克斯；Dreamworks 梦工场；Paramount Pictures Corporation 派拉蒙影片公司；20th Century Fox 二十世纪福克斯；Columbia Pictures Inc. 哥伦比亚影片公司；Disney 迪斯尼；New Line Cinema 新线电影公司

# Unit 6

## Mother and Child

*Learning Objectives:*

You Are Able to:

☞ Identify some basic sounds of letters

☞ Use proper expressions to comment on love

☞ Know the use of verb II

☞ Write letters with the correct format

You are suggested to:

☞ Be familiar with true love between parents and children

• Unit 6  Mother and Child •

*It is God who cannot be present everywhere; therefore he created mothers. A mother's love is something that no one can explain, and nothing can destroy it or take that love away. It is made of deep devotion and sacrifice and pain; it is endless and unselfish and enduring. The relationship between a mother and a child is very special and that is as good as truth. Each child is obliged to hold the greatest emotional bond with his/her mother, for better for worse, for richer for poorer, in sickness and in health, to love, honor, and cherish.*

## Part I  Phonetics

### Task 1  Identifying Their Pronunciations

*Directions: Listen to the following words and read after the speaker, paying attention to the colored parts.*

| /iː/ | /ɪ/ | /ɛ/ | /a/ | /əː/ | /ə/ | /ʌ/ | /uː/ | /ʊ/ | /ɔː/ | /ɒ/ | /ɑː/ |
| /eɪ/ | /ʌɪ/ | /ɔɪ/ | /əʊ/ | /aʊ/ | /ɪə/ | /ɛː/ | /uə/ |
| /p/ | /b/ | /t/ | /d/ | /k/ | /g/ | /f/ | /v/ | /s/ | /z/ | /ʃ/ | /ʒ/ | /h/ | /r/ |
| /tʃ/ | /dʒ/ | /m/ | /n/ | /ŋ/ | /l/ | /w/ | /j/ | /tr/ | /dr/ | /ts/ | /dz/ | /w/ | /j/ |

(1) cup       picture    class      color
(2) nice      pencil     license    twice
(3) green     game       bag        fog
(4) age       language   manager    garage
(5) see       speak      sky        straight
(6) hers      business   because    noodles
(7) three     through    bath       thumb
(8) them      with       theirs     though
(9) which     what       white      wink
(10) who      whose      whole      whom

*Practice: Write down the sound of the underlined part of the words.*

bri<u>dge</u>  h<u>air</u>  <u>k</u>nife  on<u>i</u>on  r<u>ou</u>nd

## Task 2   Appreciating a Poem

*Directions: Listen to the poem written by Robert Frost "Stopping by Woods on a Snowy Evening". Choose the words you hear to fill in the blanks.*

| wood | /wʊd/ | n. | 木,木材,木柴,树林,林地 |
| fill | /fɪl/ | v. | (使)充满,(使)装满,填满 |
| queer | /kwɪə/ | adj. | 古怪的,可疑的 |
| frozen | /ˈfrəʊzn/ | adj. | 冷冻的,冷藏的,凝结的,(水或雪)结冰的 |
| harness | /ˈhɑːnɪs/ | n. | 马具,挽具 |
| | | v. | 给(马等)装上挽具 |
| sweep | /swiːp/ | v. | 扫,打扫,拂去 |
| downy | /ˈdaʊnɪ/ | adj. | 绒毛的,柔和的,多丘岗的,丘原的 |
| promise | /ˈprɒmɪs/ | n. | 承诺,诺言 |
| | | v. | 允诺,答应 |

---

**Poem     Stopping by Woods on a Snowy Evening**

*Robert Frost*

Whose woods these are I think I know.
His _____ (house, horse) is in the village though;
He will not _____ (say, see) me stopping here
To watch his woods _____ (feel, fill) up with snow.
My _____ (litter, little) horse must think it queer
To stop without a farmhouse near
Between the woods and frozen lake
The darkest evening of the year.
He gives his harness bells a _____ (shake, snake)
To ask if there is _____ (thumb, some) mistake.
The only other sound's the sweep

> Of easy wind and downy _____ (flake, flak).
> The woods are lovely, dark and deep,
> But I have promises to keep,
> And _____ (miles, mills) to go before I sleep,
> And miles to go before I sleep.

### Task 3   Time for Fun: Tongue Twisters

*Directions: Practise the tongue twisters sentence by sentence after the speaker. Pay attention to the sounds.*

(1) Give papa a cup of proper coffee in a copper coffee cup.

(2) I thought a thought. But the thought I thought wasn't the thought I thought I thought.

(3) When the wind is in the East, it's good neither for man nor beast; when the wind is in the North, the skillful fisher goes not forth; when the wind is in the south, it blows the bait in the fish's mouth; when the wind is in the west, then it's in its very best.

## Part II   Listening and Speaking

### Task 1   Short Dialogues

*Directions: Listen to the following short dialogues and fill in the blanks with the information you get from the recording. Each dialogue will be read twice.*

(1) **W:** Why don't you give up _____? It's such a bad _____ to the children.
   **M:** It's one of the real _____ in my life. That's why.

(2) **M:** Helen, have you thought we should _____ down and start a family?
   **M:** Do you mean I have to _____ my job and stay at home all day long looking after the _____ and _____?

(3) **W:** Last year I paid a _____ to China and I was deeply _____ by the Great Wall, the delicious Chinese food and the relationship between Chinese children and their parents.
   **M:** Do you think parents in the United States and China _____ in their _____ to parenting?

(4) **W:** Tom, what are you _____ in your hand?
   **M:** It's my family photo _____.

(5) **W:** Why did your _____ make you stay at home last night?
   **M:** They wanted to go out, and so they made me _____ my baby brother.

### Task 2  Answering the Questions

*Directions: You will hear 5 recorded questions. Listen carefully and choose the proper answer to each question. The questions will be read twice.*

(1) A. Mark doesn't like eating more.
    B. Mark is devising a weight-loss program.
    C. Mark is probable not eating enough.
    D. Mark is in hospital.

(2) A. The generation gap.     B. The daughter disobeys.
    C. The father's troubles.    D. The father's family.

(3) A. At 8      B. At 9      C. At 10      D. At 11

(4) A. To get married.        B. To go to the exhibition.
    C. To attend a wedding.    D. To attend a party.

(5) A. Inside a bookstore.     B. Outside an art museum.
    C. Outside a sports centre.  D. In a theatre.

### Task 3  Oral Practice

*Warm-Up 1: Match the expressions in the left column with the expressions in the right column so as to form 7 short dialogues.*

| | |
|---|---|
| (1) —What love do you think is the greatest in the world? | —Seven years. |
| (2) —How many people are there in your family? | —Yes, I have a large and harmonious family. |
| (3) —How long have you been married? | —Six. |
| (4) —Nancy, meet my family members: my father, my mother ... | —She is a nurse. |
| (5) —How lovely your son is ! | —Thank you. He is a little naughty. |
| (6) —What's your daughter? | —Mother's love , of course. |
| (7) —Are your grandparents living with you all? | —Pleased to meet you. What a big family you have! |

# Unit 6  Mother and Child

*Warm-Up 2: Work with your partner to praltise the following useful expressions.*

**If you introduce your family to your friend, you can say**

(1) This is my family.

(2) There are ...people in my family.

(3) They're my grandfather, grandmother...

(4) My grandfather is an engineer.

**If you are the friend visiting a family, you can say**

(1) Nice to meet you.

(2) Could you please show me your family photo album?

(3) Can you tell me the woman who is next to you?

(4) What a warm family it is!

**Dialogue**

*Sally and Tom are talking about Tom's family photo album. The conversation is as follows:*

Sally: Tom, what are you holding in your hand?

Tom: It's my family photo album.

Sally: May I have a look at it?

Tom: Sure.

Sally: Is this old gentleman your grandfather?

Tom: No, he is my great-grandfather.

Sally: Is the old lady sitting beside him, your great grandmother?

Tom: Yes, you are right.

Sally: Can you show me the photo of your parents?

Tom: Just turn over the page and you'll see it.

Sally: Oh, what a handsome gentleman your father is! And your mother is a good match for your father. How many brothers and sisters do you have?

Tom: I have one elder brother and two younger sisters.

Sally: Are your grandparents living with you all?

Tom: Yes.

Sally: Oh, Tom, how I envy you! You have such a large and harmonious family!

### New Words and Expressions

| album | /ˈalbəm/ | n. | 粘贴簿,集邮簿,相册 |
| --- | --- | --- | --- |
| beside | /bɪˈsʌɪd/ | prep. | (表示位置)在……旁边 |
| handsome | /ˈhans(ə)m/ | adj. | (男子)英俊的 |
| match | /matʃ/ | n. | 相似之物,相配之物 |
| harmonious | /hɑːˈməʊnɪəs/ | adj. | 和谐的,和睦的,协调的,调和的 |

## Task 4　Role Play

(1) Imagine you are from America, and try to make some introductions of your family to your American friend. Make up a dialogue between you and your friend. The patterns you learned just now and the expressions given below may be of some help to you.

### Expressions

There are five people in my family.
我们家有五个人。

My mother is a teacher. My father is ...
我妈妈是教师,我爸爸是……

Can I have a look at your family photo album?
我能看一下你的全家福吗?

(2) Now you and your friend Mary are discussing the role of a woman at home. You hold different opinions on this issue. Make up a dialogue according to the information. The patterns you learned just now and the expressions given below may be of some help to you.

### Expressions

| marriage | /ˈmarɪdʒ/ | n. | 结婚,婚姻 |
| --- | --- | --- | --- |
| housework | /ˈhaʊswəːk/ | n. | 家务劳动 |
| boring | /ˈbɔːrɪŋ/ | adj. | 无趣的,单调的,乏味的 |

## Task 5　Leisure Time: Learning to Sing a Song

1. Listen to the song "Only You".
2. Listen to the song again and fill in the missing words.

• Unit 6　Mother and Child •

## Only You

Only you can make all this world seem _____.
Only you can make the _____ bright.
Only you and you alone can thrill me like you do.
And fill my heart with love for only you.
Only you can make this _____ in me.
For it's true you are my destiny.
When you hold my hand, I understand.
The _____ that you do.
You're my dream come true.
My one and only you.
Only you can make this change in me.
For it's true you are my destiny.
When you hold my hand, I understand.
The magic that you do.
You're my dream come _____.
My one and only you

3. Learn to sing the song after the singer.

## Part III　Reading

### Text A

### A True Gift of Love
*Anonymous*

"Can I see my baby?" the happy new mother asked.

When she looked upon his tiny face, she gasped. The baby had been born without ears.

Time proved that the baby's hearing was perfect. It was only his appearance that was marred. When he rushed home from school one day and flung himself into his mother's arms, she sighed, knowing that his life was to be a succession of heartbreaks.

He blurted out the tragedy. "A boy, a big boy ... called me a freak."

He grew up, handsome for his misfortune. A favorite with his fellow students, he might have been class president, but for that. He developed a talent for literature and music. His mother felt a kindness in her heart.

The boy's father had a session with the family physician. "Could nothing be done?"

"I believe I could transplant a pair of outer ears, if they could be obtained," the doctor decided. Then the search began for a person who would make such a sacrifice for a young man.

Two years went by. One day, his father said to the son, "You're going to the hospital, son. Mother and I have someone who will donate the ears you need. But it's a secret."

The operation was a brilliant success, and a new person emerged. His talents blossomed into genius, and school and college became a series of triumphs.

Later he married and entered the diplomatic service. One day, he asked his father, "Who gave me the ears? I could never do enough for him or her."

"I do not believe you could," said the father, "but the agreement was that you are not to know."

The years kept their secret, but the day did come. One of the darkest days ever passed through a son. He stood with his father over his mother's casket. Slowly, tenderly, the father stretched forth a hand

and raised the thick, reddish brown hair to reveal the mother had no outer ears.

"Mother said she was glad she never let her hair be cut," his father whispered gently, "and nobody ever thought mother less beautiful, did they?"

### New Words

| | | | |
|---|---|---|---|
| anonymous | /əˈnɒnɪməs/ | adj. | 匿名的 |
| ☆gasp | /gɑːsp/ | v. | 气喘吁吁地说；喘着气说话 |
| ★appearance | /əˈpɪər(ə)ns/ | n. | 外貌 |
| ☆mar | /mɑː/ | v. | 毁坏 |
| fling | /flɪŋ/ | v. | 猛冲 |
| sigh | /sʌɪ/ | v. | 叹气 |
| ☆succession | /səkˈsɛʃ(ə)n/ | n. | 接连，一系列 |
| blurt | /bləːt/ | v. | 脱口而出 |
| freak | /friːk/ | n. | 怪人 |
| misfortune | /mɪsˈfɔːtʃuːn, -tʃ(ə)n/ | n. | 不幸 |
| ☆session | /ˈsɛʃ(ə)n/ | n. | （进行某活动连续的）一段时间 |
| physician | /fɪˈzɪʃ(ə)n/ | n. | 内科医师 |
| ☆transplant | /transˈplɑːnt, trɑːns-, -nz-/ | v. | 移植 |
| obtain | /əbˈteɪn/ | v. | 获得；流行 |
| sacrifice | /ˈsakrɪfʌɪs/ | v. | 奉献，牺牲 |
| donate | /də(ʊ)ˈneɪt/ | v. | 捐献 |
| ★emerge | /ɪˈməːdʒ/ | v. | 出现 |

# Unit 6  Mother and Child

| blossom | /ˈblɒs(ə)m/ | v. | 长成,繁荣 |
| --- | --- | --- | --- |
| triumph | /ˈtraɪʌmf/ | n. | 胜利 |
| diplomatic | /dɪpləˈmatɪk/ | adj. | 外交上的 |
| casket | /ˈkɑːskɪt/ | n. | 棺材 |
| stretch | /stretʃ/ | v. | 伸展 |
| ★whisper | /ˈwɪspə/ | v. | 低声说 |

## Phrases and Expressions

| look upon | 端详,凝视 |
| --- | --- |
| a succession of | 一连串 |
| blurt out | 脱口而出 |
| make a sacrifice for | 为……做出牺牲 |
| a brilliant success | 非常成功 |
| blossom into | 长成,出落成 |
| pass through | 度过,经历 |

## Exercises

*Directions: Answer the following questions according to the passage.*

1. What's wrong with the new-born baby?
2. Why did the boy rush into home and fling himself into his mother's arms?
3. Did the boy become a class president? Why or why not?
4. What was the family physician's decision after the father had a session with him?
5. What happened to the boy after the operation?
6. When did the boy find the secret of the donator?
7. Who donated the ears to the boy?

*Directions: Choose the best meaning of each italicized word according to the context and try to tell how you get the answer.*

1. It was only his *appearance* that was marred.
   A. 外貌    B. 表象    C. 表现
2. Then the search began for a person who would make such a *sacrifice* for a young man.
   A. 祭品    B. 贡献    C. 牺牲
3. Mother and I have someone who will *donate* the ears you need. But it's a secret.
   A. 捐赠    B. 投入    C. 贡献
4. Later he married and entered the *diplomatic* service.
   A. 外交的    B. 外贸的    C. 交际的
5. The father *stretched* forth a hand and raised the thick, reddish brown hair to reveal the mother had no outer ears.
   A. 延伸    B. 伸出    C. 伸展

129

## Vocabulary

*Directions: Match each word in Column A with its definition in Column B*

| Column A | Column B |
|---|---|
| 1. appearance | a. give up on something |
| 2. fling | b. give money, food, etc, especially to charity |
| 3. stretch | c. what someone / something appears to be |
| 4. whisper | d. move (oneself or part of one's body) suddenly |
| 5. donate | e. great achievement or success |
| 6. sigh | f. related to or involving the work of diplomats |
| 7. diplomatic | g. to breathe in and out making a long sound, especially because you are bored, disappointed, tired etc. |
| 8. genius | h. speak softly or gently |
| 9. sacrifice | i. extend or thrust out (a limb or part of the body) |
| 10. triumph | j. very high level of intelligence, mental skill, or ability |

*Directions: Complete the following sentences with words from Column A above. Change the form where necessary.*

1. She _____ herself in front of the car.
2. It is unwise for Mary to _____ her career for her husband.
3. Organ transition is one of the _____ of modern medicine.
4. The two countries established _____ relations last year.
5. He _____ with despair at the thought of all the chances he had missed.
6. Einstein is a _____ as a scientist.
7. He _____ out his arms to take the book.
8. The child _____ a word in his mum's ear.
9. Last year he _____ $1000 to the AIDS research.
10. We can't judge a person from his or her _____.

*Directions: Translate the following sentences into English.*

1. _____(连续的失败) made him depressed.
2. Tom _____(脱口说出) the secret.
3. She _____ (已经成为了) a beautiful girl.
4. He _____( 经历了) a lot of difficulties.
5. The old man _____(捐赠了巨款) to the Red Cross.

## Text B

### The Meanest Mother
*Bobbie Pingaro*

I had the meanest mother in the whole world. When others had cokes and candy for lunch, I had to eat a sandwich. As you can guess, my supper was different from the other kids' also.

My mother insisted upon knowing where we were at all times. She had to know who our friends were and where we were going. She insisted if we said we'd be gone an hour, that we be gone one hour or less—not one hour and one minute.

We had to wear clean clothes and take a bath every day. The other kids always wore their clothes for days. We reached the height of insults because she made our clothes herself, just to save money.

The worst is yet to come. We had to be in bed by nine each night and up at eight the next morning. We couldn't sleep till noon like our friends. So while they slept—my mother actually had the nerve to break the *Child Labor Law*. We had to wash dishes, make beds and all sorts of cruel things. Through the years, things didn't improve a bit. We could not lie in bed and miss school. Our marks in school had to be up to par. Our friends' report cards had beautiful colors on them, black for passing, red for failing. My mother, being as different as she was, would settle for nothing less than ugly black marks.

My mother was a complete failure as a mother. Out of four children, a couple of us attained some higher education. None of us have ever been arrested or divorced. Each of my brothers served his time in the service of this country. She forced us to grow up into God-fearing, educated, honest adults. Using this as a background, I am now trying to raise my three children. I am filled with pride when my children call me mean. Why? Because now I thank God every day for giving me the meanest mother in the whole world.

## New Words

| | | | |
|---|---|---|---|
| mean | /miːn/ | adj. | 吝啬的,自私的 |
| sandwich | /ˈsan(d)wɪdʒ, -wɪtʃ/ | n. | 三明治 |
| ★ insult | /ɪnˈsʌlt/ | n. | 侮辱 |
| actually | /ˈaktjʊəli, -tʃʊ-/ | adv. | 实际上 |
| nerve | /nəːv/ | n. | 勇气 |
| cruel | /krʊəl/ | adj. | 残酷的,残忍的 |
| attain | /əˈteɪn/ | v. | 达到 |
| arrest | /əˈrɛst/ | v. | 逮捕,拘捕 |
| ★ divorce | /dɪˈvɔːs/ | v. | 离婚 |
| God-fearing | | adj. | 虔诚的,敬神的 |
| raise | /reɪz/ | v. | 抚养,饲养 |

## Phrases and Expressions

| | |
|---|---|
| make beds | 铺床 |
| up to par | 达到高水平 |
| settle for | 满足于 |
| serve one's time | 服兵役 |
| grow up | 长大,成熟 |
| be filled with | 充满着 |

## Proper Names

| | |
|---|---|
| Child Labor Law | 童工法 |

# Exercises

*Directions: Decide whether the following statements are true (T) or false (F) according to the information in the passage.*

1. We had the same supper as the other kids'.　　( )
2. My mother actually had the nerve to break the Child Labor Law.　　( )
3. My mother could forgive our beautiful color report cards.　　( )
4. I am now trying to raise my three children like my mother.　　( )
5. My mother forced us to grow up into God-fearing, educated, honest adults.　　( )
6. I don't like to be called "mean" by my children.　　( )
7. I thank God every day for giving me the meanest mother in the whole world.　　( )

## Unit 6  Mother and Child

*Directions: Guess the meanings of the words and phrases in the box according to the passage. Then, use them to complete the following sentences, changing the form if necessary.*

| help a bit | up to par | make beds | grow up |
|---|---|---|---|
| serve one's time | be filled with | be so mean to | |

1. My life _____ pleasure.
2. Don't _____ your colleagues.
3. I can lend you 100 yuan, if you want. That should _____ .
4. I don't think her performance was _____ .
5. Each of adult males should _____ in the service of the country.
6. They are old enough to _____ for themselves.
7. Their children have all _____ and left home now.

*Directions: Pay attention to different parts of speech and select the appropriate word to fill in the blanks.*

1. high    highly    height    heighten
   a. It's _____ unlikely that she'll be late.
   b. The rooms had _____ ceilings.
   c. It is almost 3 metres in _____ .
   d. The campaign is intended to _____ public awareness of the disease.

2. mean    means    meaning
   a. What did he _____ by that remark?
   b. She's always been _____ with money.
   c. Computer is an effective _____ of communication.
   d. Words often have several _____ .

3. pride    proud    proudly
   a. I take a _____ in my work.
   b. He was _____ of himself for not giving up.
   c. She _____ displayed her prize.

4. attain    attainment    attainable
   a. Most of our students _____ five "A" grades in their exams.
   b. The _____ of his ambitions was still a dream.
   c. This standard is easily _____ by most students.

*Directions: First translate the following English sentences into Chinese. Then, pay attention to the italicized parts in the English sentences and translate the Chinese sentences by simulating the structure of the English sentences.*

1. *While* other kids ate candy for breakfast, I had to have cereal, eggs or toast.
   吉姆很擅长理科,而他的兄弟绝对是不可救药。

2. *As* you can guess, my supper was different from the other kids also.
   正如你所猜测的,他在会上一言不发。

3. We reached the height of insults *because* she made our clothes herself, just to save money.
   是他吩咐我才做的。

4. We could*n't* sleep *till* noon like our friends.
   难道你就不能像我父母一样等我们回到家吗?

5. *None of us* have ever been arrested or divorced.
   这些钢笔一支都不能用。

6. Because now I *thank* God every day *for* giving me the meanest mother in the whole world.
   我得写信感谢玛丽送给我这份礼物。

**Directions: Group activity.**

Work in groups to discuss the image of the writer's mother, using the following words to describe the personality of a perfect mother in your mind.

> caring, patient, diligent, warm-hearted, kind, understanding, nice, modest, brave, trustworthy, thoughtful, creative, great, loyal, mean, strict, selflessness

## Part IV  Grammar

### 动词Ⅱ  动词的时态和语态

**一、动词的时态**

英语的动词常用的有12种时态,分别是:一般时态——一般现在时、一般过去时、一般将来时;完成时态——现在完成时、过去完成时、将来完成时;进行时态——现在进行时、过去进行时、将来进行时;完成进行时——现在完成进行时、过去完成进行时、将来完成进行时。

**(一)一般时态**

1. 一般现在时

(1) 一般现在时表示没有时限的持久存在的动作或状态或现阶段反复发生的动作或状态,常和副词 usually, often, always, sometimes, regularly, near, occasionally, every year, every week 等连用。如:

1) The moon moves around the earth.

2) Mr. Smith travels to work by bus every day.

(2) 在由 after, until, before, once, when, even if, in case, as long as, as soon as, the moment 以及 if, unless 等引导的时间状语从句或条件状语从句中,通常用一般现在时代替将来

时。如：

1) I will tell him the news as soon as I see him.

2) I will not go to countryside if it rains tomorrow.

(3) 某些表示起始的动词,可用一般现在时表示按规定、计划或安排要发生的动作,这类动词有：be, go, come, start, depart, arrive, begin, leave 等。如：

1) The plane leaves at three sharp.

2) The new teachers arrive tomorrow.

2. 一般过去时

(1) 表示过去某一特定时间所发生的、可完成的动作或状态,常与表示确切过去时间的词、短语或从句连用。如：

We went to the pictures last night and saw a very interesting film.

(2) 表示过去习惯性动作。如：

1) He always went to class last.

2) I used to do my homework in the library.

3. 一般将来时

(1) 表示将来打算进行或期待发生的动作或状态。如：

I shall graduate next year.

(2) 几种替代形式：

1) be going to +v 在口语中广泛使用,表示准备做或将发生的事情。如：

I'm going to buy a house when we've saved enough money.

2) be to +v 表示计划安排要做的事,具有"必要"的强制性意义。如：

I am to play tennis this afternoon.

3) be about to +v 表示即将发生的事情。如：

He was about to start.

(二) 进行时态

1. 现在进行时

(1) 表示现在正在进行的动作,常与 now, right now, at the moment, for the time being, for the present 等连用。如：

Don't disturb her. She is reading a newspaper now.

(2) 表示现阶段经常发生的动作,常与 always, continually, forever, constantly 等连用。如：

My father is forever criticizing me.

(3) 表示根据计划或安排在最近要进行的事情。具有这种语法功能的动词仅限于过渡性动词,即表示从一个状态或位置转移到另一个状态或位置上去的动词。常用的有：go, come, leave, start, arrive, return 等。如：

They are leaving for Hong Kong next month.

(4) 有些动词不能用进行时,这是一类表示"感觉,感情,存在,从属"等的动词。如：see, hear, smell, taste, feel, notice, look, appear (表示感觉的动词); hate, love, fear, like, want,

wish,prefer,refuse,forgive(表示感情的动词);be,exist,remain,stay,obtain(表示存在状态的动词);have,possess,own,contain,belong,consist of,form(表示占有与从属的动词);understand,know,believe,think,doubt,forget,remember(表示思考理解的动词)。但是如果它们词义改变,便也可用进行时态。如:

1) Tom looks pale. What's wrong with him?

（look 在此为联系动词,意为"显得,看上去"）

2) Tom is looking for his books.

（look 在此为实义动词,意为"寻找"）

2. 过去进行时

过去进行时表示一个过去的动作发生时或发生后,另一个过去的动作正在进行,或表示过去反复的习惯,常与 always,continually,constantly 等动词连用。如:

1) We were discussing the matter when the headmaster entered.

2) Whenever I visited him, he was always writing at the desk.

3. 将来进行时

将来进行时主要表示将来某一时刻正在进行的动作,或表示要在将来某一时刻开始,并继续下去的动作。常用来表示礼貌的询问、请求等。如:

1) This time next day they will be sitting in the cinema.

2) What will you be doing at six tomorrow evening?

（三）完成时态

完成时态通常表示已完成或从事的动作。它可分为:

1. 现在完成时

（1）现在完成时用来表示对目前状况仍有影响的,刚刚完成的动作(常与 yet,already,just 连用),或者过去某一时刻发生的,持续到现在的情况(常与 for,since 连用)。如:

1) I have just finished my homework.

2) Mary has been ill for three days.

（2）常与现在完成时连用的时间状语有 since,for,during,over 等引导出的短语;副词 already,yet,just,ever,now,before,often,lately,recently 等;状语词组 this week (morning,month,year),so far,up to now,many times,up to the present 等。如:

1) I haven't been there for five years.

2) So far, she hasn't enjoyed the summer vacation.

3) There have been a lot of changes since 1978.

2. 过去完成时

（1）表示过去某时间前已经发生的动作或情况,这个过去的时间可以用 by,before 等介词短语或一个时间状语从句来表示;或者表示一个动作在另一个过去动作之前已经完成。如:

1) We had just had our breakfast when Tom came in.

2) By the end of last year they had turned out 5,000 bicycles.

（2）过去完成时常用于以下固定句型：

    1) hardly, scarcely, barely + 过去完成时 + when + 过去时。如：

       Hardly had I got on the bus when it started to move.

    2) no sooner + 过去完成时 + than + 过去时。如：

       No sooner had I gone out than he came to see me.

    3) by (the end of) + 过去时间，主句中谓语动词用过去完成时。如：

       The experiment had been finished by 4 o'clock yesterday afternoon.

3. 将来完成时

将来完成时表示在将来某一时刻将完成或在另一个未来的动作发生之前已经完成的动作；也可以用来表示一种猜测。常与将来完成时连用的时间状语有 by (the time / the end of) + 表示将来时间的短语和句子；before (the end of) + 表示将来时间的词语或句子；when, after 等加上表示将来动作的句子等。如：

1) By this time tomorrow you will have arrived in Shanghai.

2) I shall have finished this composition before 9 o'clock.

3) When we get on the railway station, the train will probably have left.

（四）完成进行时

完成进行时是完成时的强调形式，有现在完成进行时，过去完成进行时，将来完成进行时。

1. 现在完成进行时

表示过去某一时刻开始的动作或状态一直延续到现在。如：

I have been looking for my lost book for three days, but I still haven't found it.

2. 过去完成进行时

表示过去某一时刻之前开始的动作或状态一直延续到过去某一时刻。如：

It had been raining cats and dogs for over a week and the downpour had caused landslides in many places.

3. 将来完成进行时

表示在将来某一时刻之前开始的一个动作或状态一直延续到将来某一时刻。如：

By the time you arrive tonight, she will have been typing for hours.

## 二、动词的被动语态

### （一）被动语态的构成

以动词 do 为例，主动语态和被动语态的结构形式列表如下：

| 时态 | 主动语态 | 被动语态 |
|---|---|---|
| 一般现在时 | do/does | am/is/are done |
| 现在进行时 | am/is/are doing | am/is/are being done |
| 现在完成时 | have/has done | have/has been done |
| 一般将来时 | will/shall do | will/shall be done |
| 过去将来时 | would/should do | would/should be done |
| 一般过去时 | did | was/were done |
| 过去进行时 | was/were doing | was/were being done |
| 过去完成时 | had done | had been done |
| 情态动词 | can/may/must/should/would do | can/may/must/should/would be done |

**特别提示:**

主动语态变为被动语态时,其时态不变。

**(二) 被动语态的用法**

(1) 当不知道谁是动作的执行者,或者没有必要指出谁是动作的执行者时,通常用被动语态。如:

This computer was made in China. 这台计算机是中国制造的。

More trees must be planted. 必须种更多的树。

(2) 当需要强调动作的承受者而不是执行者时,通常用被动语态。如:

English is spoken in many parts of the world. 世界许多地方讲英语。

The book is read by all classes of people. 这本书社会各阶层的人都读。

(3) 为了强调动作的执行者而用by修饰时,通常用被动语态。如:

The window was broken by the boy who lives next door. 窗子是住在隔壁的男孩打破的。

Such songs are usually sung by girls. 这些歌通常是女孩唱的。

(4) 为使语气婉转,避免提及自己或对方而使用被动语态,或由于修辞的需要使用被动语态使句子得以更好安排。

The new task must be finished by the end of next week. 必须在下周之前完成这项新的任务。

# Exercises

*Directions: There are 15 incomplete statements here. You are required to complete each statement by choosing the appropriate answer from the 4 choices marked A, B, C and D.*

1. That day he _____ his clothes before he came to see me.

   A. has washed    B. washed    C. had been washing    D. was washed

2. —I haven't finished my composition.
   —I_____ for two hours and a half.
   A. have written it          B. have been writing it
   C. wrote it                 D. am writing it
3. I will take my daughter with me when I_____ Shanghai.
   A. go to         B. will go to       C. have been to        D. have gone to
4. This bright girl_____ the truth in front of the enemy.
   A. didn't say               B. couldn't speak to
   C. said                     D. didn't tell
5. The bridge which_____ last year looks really beautiful.
   A. was built     B. built            C. was set up          D. had been built
6. —When_____ school begin?
   —Next Monday.
   A. has           B. does             C. did                 D. is going to
7. I will_____ here till you give me some money.
   A. leave         B. not leave        C. come                D. return
8. I_____ here since I moved here.
   A. will work                B. worked
   C. work                     D. have been working
9. Every time I_____ there, I will buy him something nice.
   A. went          B. will go          C. go                  D. have gone
10. It was said that his father_____.
    A. has died     B. died             C. has been dead       D. had died
11. When he_____ all the newspapers, he'll go home.
    A. sells        B. has sold         C. will have sold      D. will be sold
12. "Where_____ the recorder? I can't see it anywhere." "I_____ it right here. But now it's gone."
    A. did you put/have put     B. have you put/put
    C. had you put/was putting  D. were you putting/have put
13. By this time next year he_____ from the college.
    A. will be graduating       B. should be graduating
    C. will have graduated      D. is graduating
14. The pencil_____ well.
    A. writes       B. is written       C. was written         D. writing
15. Every possible means_____, but none prove successful.
    A. has tried    B. has been tried   C. is being tried      D. tried

# Part V  Applied Writing

## Letters (书信)

书信是重要的交际工具。英文书信分为私人书信和公务书信两大类。公务书信是单位与单位或单位与个人之间来往的信件;私人书信是指亲戚朋友之间的通信。依据习惯,英文书信大体都由六部分组成,即:信头(heading)、信内地址(inside address)、称呼(salutation)、正文(body)、结尾语(complimentary close)和签名(signature)。

### a. 信头 (heading)

信头包括发信人的地址和发信的具体日期两部分。信头放在信纸的右上角,一般分行写出。要先写发信人地址,再写发信的日期。写地址时依据从小到大的原则,通常第一行写门牌号和街名,第二行写地区名和邮政编码,第三行是国名,第四行是日期。日期的顺序是"日-月-年(英式)",也可是"月-日-年(美式)"。

一般信头每行末不用标点符号,但每行中间应用的标点不可少,城区名和邮政编码之间,日月和年份之间要用逗号隔开。

信头的书写格式有两种:并列式和斜列式。并列式是指信头各行开头上下排列整齐,而斜列式是下一行开头较上一行的开头向右移一至两个字母的位置。

### b. 信内地址 (inside address)

信内地址包括收信人的姓名和地址两部分。在公务信件中要写明这一项,在私人信件中,这一项常常省略。信内地址的位置位于信头的左下方,它的开始行低于信头的结尾行,位于信纸中央的左边。格式与寄信人地址一样。

### c. 称呼 (salutation)

称呼是对收信人称谓,自成一行,与信内地址上下排齐。在称呼后,英国人常用逗号,美国人则常用冒号。在私人信件中可直呼收信人的名字,但公务信件中一定要写收信人的姓或职位头衔。大部分信件在称呼前加"Dear",如:Dear Professor / Prof. Bergon / Dear Dr. Johnson。对不相识的人可按性别称呼,如:Dear Sir, Dear Madam。如果不知道收信人的性别则可用Dear Sir or Madam 或 To whom it may concern。

### d. 正文 (body)

正文是书信的核心部分。正文的写作必须注意以下几点:

(1) 正文从低于称呼一至二行处写起,每段第一行向内缩进约五个字母,转行顶格。正文也可采用并列式的写法,即每行都顶格,但段与段之间中间要空出两三行表示分段。

(2) 信的内容中的每个段落,只能有一个中心思想。为了表达的清楚,还要尽可能地用短句,少用长句、难句。段落也宜短不宜长,尤其开头和结尾两段更应简短。

(3) 书信的第一句话或第一段,通常被称为起首语。一般说来,人们习惯用一些客套的写法作为书信正文的起始,即先将对方来信的日期、主题加以简单描述,以便对方一看便知该信是回答哪封信的。如果是第一次给对方写信,也可用开头语作必要的自我介绍,并表明自己写信的主要目的。

### e. 结尾语 (complimentary close)

结尾语就是结尾的客套语。一般写于正文下空一两行后,从信纸中央处起笔写,第一个字母大写,末尾用逗号。结尾语措辞的变化依据情况而定,通常有以下几种:

(1) 写给单位、团体或不相识的人的信:

Yours (very) truly, (Very) Truly yours,

Yours (very) faithfully, (Very) Faithfully yours,

(2) 写给尊长上级的信:

Yours (very) respectfully, Yours (very) obediently,

Yours gratefully, Yours appreciatively,

也可以将 Yours 放在后面。

(3) 写给熟人或朋友的信:

Yours, Yours ever, Yours fraternally,

Yours cordially, Yours devotedly,

也可以将 Yours 放在后面。

(4) 给亲戚或密友的信:

Yours, Yours ever, Yours affectionately,

Yours devoted friend, Lovingly yours,

Yours loving son (father, mother, nephew...),

以上各种情况 yours 无论放在前面或是放在后面都行,但不可缩写或省去。

### f. 签名 (signature)

签名是在结尾客套语的下面,稍偏于右,这样末一个字可以接近空白而和上面的正文一样齐。签名应当由写信人手写完成,手写后可附打印的全名。写信人为女性,则可在署名前用括号注明 Mrs. 或 Miss。男子签字前不可用 Mr.、Prof. 或 Dr. 字样。

### 【格式】

#### A. 齐头式 (Block Format)

_____ (信头)

_____

_____ (日期)

_____ (信内地址)

_____

_____(称呼)

_____

_____

_____(正文)

_____(结束语)

_____(签名)

B. 缩进式（Indented Format）

_____(信头)

_____(日期)

_____(信内地址)

_____(称呼)

_____

_____

_____(正文)

_____(结束语)

_____(签名)

## Basic Expressions（常用表达）

☆ It is so great to hear from you again.

☆ It is a great pleasure for me to...

☆ With great delight I learned that...

☆ I must apologize for not writing to you sooner.

☆ I am sorry that it has taken me so long to reply..., but...

☆ Best regards to you and your family.

☆ Please say hello for me to ...

# Unit 6　Mother and Child

◆ **英文书信信封的写法**

英文书信信封的写法同中文也不一样。具体来讲,英文书信应这样安排信封内容。

1. 寄信人姓名地址写在信封的左上角,也可写在信封的背面。收信人的姓名地址写在信封中间靠下或靠右地方。第一行写姓名,下面写地址。地址的写法同信头(heading)和信内地址(inside address)一样。所用格式(并列式或斜列式)也同信内的安排一致。注意写上邮政编码。

2. 信封左下角可以写些说明语。如写上 General Delivery (平信)、Registered (挂号信)、Express (快件)、Air mail (航空)、Personal (亲启)、Please Forward (请较交)、Printed Matter (印刷品)、Book Post (图书邮件)、Manuscripts (稿件)、Photos Enclosed (内有照片)、Top Secret (绝密件)等。

3. 若信封通过邮局寄给第三者转交给收信人,则需在收信人的姓名下面写明转交人的姓名,并在前面加上 c/o(care of)。如:

　Mr. Thomas Green
　C／O Mr. William Scott

【格式】

A. 齐头式(Block Format)

```
寄信人：王伟　　　　　邮编：310010
地址：中国浙江省杭州市文化路18号
收信人：Helen Hill　　 邮编：57890
地址：加拿大多伦多国王(King)街310号
```

```
Wang Wei
18 Wenhua Road
Hangzhou, Zhejiang
310010
China

                              Stamp

                    Helen Hill
                    310 King Street
                    Toronto, 57890
                    Canada

AIR MAIL
```

## Exercises

Directions: *This part is to test your ability to do practical writing. You are allowed 30 minutes to write a letter. Suppose you are Xiao Li. Write a letter to Xiao Zhang, a roommate of yours who is a heavy smoker. You should write at least 120 words according to the suggestion given below in Chinese.*

1. 吸烟已成为宿舍的一大问题
2. 吸烟的危害
3. 建议戒烟

**A Letter to a Roommate**

March 20, 2012
Dear Xiao Zhang,

_____
_____
_____
_____
_____
_____

Yours sincerely,
Xiao Li

# Part VI  Cultural Express

## Mystery of the White Gardenia

*Marsha Arons*

Every year on my birthday, from the time I turned 12, a white gardenia (栀子花) was delivered to my house. No card or note came with it. Calls to the florist were always in vain—it was a cash purchase. After a while I stopped trying to discover the sender's identity and just delighted in the beauty of that one magical, perfect white flower nestled in soft pink tissue paper.

But I never stopped imagining who the

anonymous giver might be. Some of my happiest moments were spent daydreaming about someone wonderful and exciting but too shy or eccentric to make known his or her identity.

My mother contributed to these imaginings. She'd ask me if there is someone for whom I had done a special kindness who might be showing appreciation. Perhaps the neighbour I'd helped when she was unloading a car full of groceries. Or maybe it was the old man across the street whose mail I retrieved during the winter so he wouldn't have to venture down his icy steps. As a teenager, though, I had more fun speculating that it might be a boy. I had a crush on one who had noticed me though I didn't know him.

When I was 17, a boy broke my heart. The night he called for the last time, I cried myself to sleep. When I awoke in the morning, there was a message scribbled on my mirror in red lipstick: "Heartily know, when half-gods go, the gods arrive." I thought about that quotation from Emerson for a long time, and until my heart healed, I left it where my mother had written it. When I finally went to get the glass cleaner, my mother knew everything was all right again.

I don't remember ever slamming my door in anger at her and shouting, "You just don't understand!" because she did understand.

One month before my high-school graduation, my father died of a heart attack. My feeling ranged from grief to abandonment, fear and anger that my dad was missing some of the most important events in my life. I became completely uninterested in my upcoming graduation, the senior-class play and the prom. But my mother, in the midst of her own grief, would not hear of my skipping any of those things.

The day before my father died, my mother and I had gone shopping for a prom dress. We'd found a spectacular one. It made me feel like Scarlett O'Hara, but it was the wrong size. When my father died, I forgot about the dress.

My mother didn't. The day before the prom, I found that dress—in the right size—draped over the living-room sofa. It wasn't just delivered, still in the box. It was presented to me—beautifully, artistically, and lovingly. I didn't care if I had a new dress or not. But my mother did.

She wanted her children to feel loved and lovable, creative and imaginative, imbued with a sense that there was magic in the world and beauty even in the face of adversity. In truth, my mother wanted her children to see themselves much like the gardenia—lovely, strong and perfect—with an aura of magic and perhaps a bit of mystery.

My mother died ten days after I was married. I was 22. That was the year the gardenia stopped coming.

# 拓展

A mother's love is like a circle. It has no beginning and no ending.
母爱就像一个圆。没有起点,也没有终点。

Youth fades; love droops; the leaves of friendship fall. A mother's secret hope outlives them all.
青春会逝去;爱情会枯萎;友谊的绿叶也会凋零。而一个母亲内心的希望比它们都要长久。

A good mother is worth a hundred schoolmasters.
一位好母亲抵得上一百个教师。

God could not be everywhere and therefore he made mothers.
上帝不能无处不在,因此他创造了母亲。

If you don't know what love is, find your mother first.
如果你不懂什么是爱,找到你的妈妈就会懂了。

A son never thinks his mother ugly, and a dog never shuns its owner's home however shabby it is.
儿不嫌母丑,狗不嫌家贫。

Of all the rights of women, the greatest is to be a mother.
女性所有的权利中,最高的权利就是做一个母亲。

Real mothers know that a child's growth is not measured by height or years or grades. It is marked by the progression of Mama to Mummy to Mother.
真正的母亲都知道,孩子的成长不是用身高、年龄或年级来衡量的。它是由孩子从"妈妈"到"妈咪"到"母亲"的称呼来记录的。

A mother is she who can take the place of all others but whose place no one else can take.
母亲可以取代一切,母亲的地位却无人能够替代。

Of all the things that come in numbers—plenty of rainbows, stars in the sky, brothers, sisters, aunts, uncles, cousins—you have but one mother.
你可以有众多的事物——缤纷的彩虹,闪耀的星星,兄弟姐妹,叔伯姨舅,但是你只有一个妈妈。

A mother is not a person to lean on but a person to make leaning unnecessary.
母亲不是赖以依靠的人,而是使依靠成为不必要的人。

All I am, or can be, I owe to my angel mother.
我之所有,我之所能,都归功于我天使般的母亲。